Ludwig van Beethoven

SONGS FOR SOLO VOICE AND PIANO

From the Breitkopf & Härtel
Complete Works Edition

With new literal prose
translations of the texts

Dover Publications, Inc.

New York

Published in Canada by General Publishing Company, Ltd., 30 Lesmill Road, Don Mills, Toronto, Ontario.
Published in the United Kingdom by Constable and Company, Ltd., 10 Orange Street, London WC2H 7EG.

This Dover edition, first published in 1986, contains, unabridged and unaltered, Nos. 215 through 254 of *Serie 23. Lieder und Gesänge mit Begleitung des Pianoforte* from *Ludwig van Beethoven's Werke. Vollständige kritisch durchgesehene überall berechtigte Ausgabe. Mit Genehmigung aller Originalverleger,* originally published by Breitkopf & Härtel, Leipzig (entire set published 1862–1865). (The only items omitted from the original *Serie 23* are No. 255, "Gesang der Mönche," and No. 256, "Canons." The series and item numbers of the original do not appear in the present volume.) The translation of the texts, the table of contents, the glossary and the lists of song titles, song openings and poets are new features, prepared specially for the present edition.

The publisher is grateful to the Paul Klapper Library of Queens College for making its copy of the original available for reproduction.

Manufactured in the United States of America
Dover Publications, Inc., 31 East 2nd Street, Mineola, N.Y. 11501

Library of Congress Cataloging-in-Publication Data

Beethoven, Ludwig van, 1770–1827.
   [Songs]
   Songs for Solo voice and piano.

   From the Breitkopf & Härtel Complete works ed.
   German and Italian words.
   Reprint (in part). Originally published: Leipzig : Breitkopf & Härtel, 1865? (Ludwig van Beethoven's Werke. Serie 23).
   1. Songs with piano.
M1620.B43 D7   1986   85-755484
ISBN 0-486-25125-X (pbk.)

CONTENTS

The present volume contains most of Beethoven's solo songs (a handful of those included are actually duets or other arrangements). Canons and folksong arrangements are not included. The WoO numbers in this table of contents are the standard "Werk ohne Opuszahl" numbers assigned to Beethoven's works that were not published with opus numbers. See the 1980 *New Grove Dictionary of Music and Musicians* (or another current work on Beethoven) for further data on original dates of composition and publication, dedicatees, text authorship and other bibliographical information beyond that included in the present volume.

ALPHABETIC LIST OF SONG TITLES

ALPHABETIC LIST OF
SONG OPENINGS

ALPHABETICAL LIST
OF POETS

GLOSSARY OF GERMAN TERMS

Ausdrucksvoll: with expression; espressivo

Componirt im Jahre . . .: composed in the year . . .

Componirt im 11. Lebensjahre: composed in his eleventh year

Componirt spätestens . . .: composed . . . at the latest

Das letzte Mal: the last time

Die ersten Male: the first times (each time but the last)

Ein wenig geschwinder: a little faster

Entschlossen (und feurig): resolutely (and fierily); risoluto (e con fuoco)

Erstes Zeitmaass: first tempo

Etwas langsam(er): somewhat (more) slowly

Etwas lebhaft: somewhat vivaciously

Etwas lebhaft, doch in einer mässig geschwinden Bewegung: somewhat vivaciously, but in a moderately fast tempo

Etwas lebhaft mit leidenschaftlicher Empfindung, doch nicht zu geschwind: somewhat vivaciously with passionate feeling, but not too fast

Etwas verzögernd (bis zum ersten Zeitmaass): slowing down somewhat (until reaching the first tempo)

Feierlich und mit Andacht: solemnly and with piety

Froh und heiter, etwas lebhaft: happily and merrily, somewhat vivaciously

Frühere Bearbeitung: earlier version (or, setting)

Fürstin: Princess

Gemäss dem verschiedenen Ausdruck in den Versen piano und forte: piano and *forte* in accordance with the varying content of the verses

Geschwind doch nicht zu viel: fast, but not too much so

Geschwinder: faster

. . . Gewidmet: dedicated to . . .

Graf: Count (title of nobility)

Im vorigen Zeitmaasse: in the preceding tempo

In einer mässigen geschwinden Bewegung mit einer komischen Art gesungen: sung comically in a moderately fast tempo

In gehender Bewegung. (Mit Empfindung, jedoch entschlossen, wohl accentuirt und sprechend vorgetragen): At a walking pace [andante]. (To be performed with feeling, but resolutely, well accented and as if speaking)

In leidenschaftlicher Bewegung: in a passionate tempo

Innig vorgetragen und nicht schleppend: to be performed with deep feeling, and not dragging

Lächelnd: smilingly

Langsam (und feierlich): slowly (and solemnly)

Lebhaft, doch nicht zu sehr: vivaciously, but not too much so

Leichtlich, nicht geschliffen: with a light touch, not dragging

Leichtlich und mit Grazie vorgetragen: to be performed with a light touch and gracefully

Liebevoll: lovingly

Majestätisch und erhaben: majestically and loftily

Man nimmt jetzt die Bewegung lebhafter als das erste Mal: now the tempo is to be more lively than the first time

Mässig, jedoch nicht schleppend: moderately, but not dragging

Mässig und eher langsam als geschwind: moderately—slow rather than fast

Mit Empfindung, aber nicht zu langsam: with feeling, but not too slowly

Mit Kraft und Feuer: with strength and ardor

Mit Lebhaftigkeit, jedoch nicht in geschwindem Zeitmaasse, und scherzend vorgetragen: to be performed vivaciously—but not in a fast tempo—and with humor

Mit Nachdruck: emphatically

Muthig: courageously

Nachgelassenes Werk: posthumous work

Nach und nach etwas langsamer: gradually somewhat more slowly

Nach und nach geschwinder: gradually faster

Nicht lange aushalten: do not hold too long

Nicht zu geschwinde, angenehm und mit viel Empfindung: not too fast, pleasantly and with much feeling

Sehr bewegt: very agitatedly

Singstimme: voice

Ziemlich anhaltend: fairly steady and regular

Ziemlich geschwind: fairly fast

Ziemlich langsam (und mit Ausdruck): fairly slowly (and expressively)

Ziemlich lebhaft und entschlossen: fairly vivaciously and resolutely

TRANSLATIONS

These literal prose translations include all verbal repeats introduced by the composer insofar as such repeats are printed beneath the music in the present volume; additional stanzas printed after the music are translated just as they stand.

An die Hoffnung
(To Hope; text by Tiedge, from *Urania*)

You that so gladly take repose during sacred nights, and gently and softly spread a veil over the sorrow that tortures a tender soul, O Hope, let the patient sufferer, uplifted by you, divine that up above an angel counts his tears! O Hope, let the patient sufferer, uplifted by you, divine that up above an angel counts his tears!

When loved voices that have long since died away are silent; when memory sits in desolation beneath withered branches, then approach the place where your forsaken one mourns and, surrounded by the gloom of midnight, leans upon sunken urns; then approach the place where your forsaken one mourns and, surrounded by the gloom of midnight, leans upon sunken urns.

And if he looks up in order to denounce his fate, when the last rays depart from his days and perish, then let him, at the brink of his earthly dreams, see the rim of a cloud illumined by a nearby sun; then let him, at the brink of his earthly dreams, see the rim of a cloud illumined by a nearby sun!

Adelaide (text by Matthisson)

Your friend walks alone in the springtime garden, gently enveloped in the lovely magical light that trembles through the waving flowery branches, Adelaide! Adelaide! In the mirroring stream, in the snow of the Alps, in the golden clouds of declining day, in the fields of stars, your image, your image gleams, Adelaide! In the golden clouds of declining day, in the fields of stars, your image, your image gleams, Adelaide! Evening breezes whisper in the tender leaves, silver bells of May rustle in the grass, the brook rushes noisily by and nightingales sing; the brook rushes noisily by and nightingales sing: "Adelaide!" Evening breezes whisper in the tender leaves, silver bells of May rustle in the grass, the brook rushes noisily by and nightingales sing: "Adelaide! Adelaide!" Some day—oh, miracle! oh, miracle!—there will bloom on my grave—oh, miracle!—there will bloom on my grave a flower from the ashes of my heart, from the ashes of my heart; there will clearly shine, there will clearly shine on every purple petal, on every purple petal [the words]: "Adelaide! Adelaide!" Some day—oh, miracle!—some day—oh, miracle!—there will bloom, ah, there will bloom on my grave a flower from the ashes of my heart, a flower from the ashes of my heart; there will clearly shine, there will clearly shine on every purple petal, on every purple petal, on every purple petal: "Adelaide! Adelaide! Adelaide!"

Sechs Lieder von Gellert (Six Songs by Gellert)

1. Bitten (Requesting)

God, Your kindness extends as far as the clouds travel; You crown us with mercifulness and hasten to support us. Lord, my fortress, my rock, my treasure, hear my supplication, give heed to my words—for I wish to pray to you, for I wish to pray to you!

2. Die Liebe des Nächsten (Love for Fellow Men)

If someone says "I love God" and yet hates his brothers, he mocks God's truth and totally demolishes it. God is love and wants me to love my fellow men just as I love myself.

3. Vom Tode (On Death)

My term of life is passing, hourly I hasten toward the grave, and how long do I perhaps still have left to live? Man, think about your death! Do not delay, for one thing is needful [refers to Luke 10:42]. Do not delay, for one thing is needful. Do not delay, for one thing is needful.

4. Die Ehre Gottes aus der Natur (The Praise of God in Nature)

The heavens extol the honor of the Eternal; their resounding perpetuates His name. He is extolled by the earth, He is praised by the seas; mankind, listen to their divine words! Who bears the innumerable stars of the heavens? Who leads the sun out of its tent? It comes and shines and smiles upon us from afar, and runs its course like a hero, and runs its course like a hero.

5. Gottes Macht und Vorsehung (God's Power and Providence)

God is my song! He is the God of strength; noble is His name and great are His works, and all the heavens are His domain.

6. Busslied (Song of Repentance)

Against You alone, against You I have sinned, and have often done wrong in Your sight. You see the guilt that announces a curse to me; O God, look also upon my lamentation, my lamentation. My supplication, my sighing are not concealed from You, and my tears are laid before You. Oh, God, my God, how long must I be careworn? How long will You withdraw Yourself from me? Lord, do not deal with me according to my sins; do not requite me, do not requite me according to my guilt, my guilt. I seek for You; let me find Your face, O

God of forbearance and patience, of forbearance and patience. May it be Your will to fill me soon with Your grace, God, Father of mercifulness. Give me joy for Your name's sake; You are a God who gladly gives joy. Let me once again happily wander on Your path, and teach me Your holy law, Your holy law; teach me to act daily in accordance with Your pleasure; You are my God, I am Your servant. Lord, my protection, hasten to support me, and guide me on a level road. He hears my cries, the Lord grants what I beseech, and accepts the charge of my soul. The Lord grants what I call for, the Lord grants what I beseech, and accepts the charge of my soul.

Acht Gesänge und Lieder (Eight Songs)

1. Urians Reise um die Welt (Urian's Trip Around the World; text by Claudius)

1. When someone takes a trip, he can tell a tale. So I took my stick and hat and chose to wander. CHORUS: And you made no mistake when you did so! Tell on, Urian!

2. First I went to the North Pole; it was cold there, I can tell you! Then I thought to myself that it was better here. CHORUS.

3. In Greenland they were very happy to see me on their territory, and they set down a pitcher of blubber before me—but I let it alone. CHORUS.

4. The Eskimos are wild and big, lazy when it comes to anything worthwhile. So I called one of them a clod and got a beating. CHORUS.

5. Now I was in America! So I said to myself: "My good fellow! There is a Northwest Passage, you know: why not go through it?" CHORUS.

6. At once I took ship and set out to sea, my telescope tied tight, and looked for it [the Passage] everywhere, but failed to find it. CHORUS.

7. From here I went to Mexico—which is even farther away than Bremen. There, I thought, gold lies around like straw; why not take a sackful? CHORUS.

8. But, but, but, but how wrong a person can be! I found nothing there but sand and stones, so I left the sack lying there. CHORUS.

9. Then I bought some cold food and smoked Kiel sprats and cake, and boarded an express coach to visit Asia. CHORUS.

10. The Mogul is a great man and extremely merciful, and clever; he was just in the midst of having a tooth pulled. CHORUS.

11. "Hm!" I thought, "he has a toothache despite all his grandeur and talents! What then is the good of being the Mogul? A person can have a toothache without all that." CHORUS.

12. I gave the innkeeper my word of honor to pay him at once; and thereupon I journeyed on to China and Bengal. CHORUS.

13. To Java and Tahiti and to Africa as well; and used the opportunity to observe many cities and people. CHORUS.

14. And I found that things everywhere were just like here, I found eccentricities all over, the people exactly like us, and just as foolish. CHORUS: There is where you did very, very wrong! Tell no more, Urian!

2. Feuerfarb' (Fire Color; text by Sophie Mereau)

1. I know a color that I am so fond of, one I regard more highly than silver and gold; I like to wear it on my brow and on my clothing; and I have named it the color of truth.

2. It is true that the glowing rose blooms in a lovely, gentle form, but it soon fades. Thus it has been consecrated as the flower of love; its charm is eternal, but it withers early.

3. The blue of the sky sends noble and gentle beams; thus loyalty has been given this friendly image. But many a small cloud darkens the pure ether! In the same way cares often creep into the loyal mind.

4. The color of snow, so shining and bright, is called the color of innocence; but it does not last. It is soon darkened, that dazzling garment. In the same way innocence falls within the shadow of defamation and envy.

5. Why, you ask, do I bestow the sacred name of truth on my beloved color? Because it emits a flaming light and is protectively surrounded by calm durability.

6. It is not harmed by the dampening rain shower, nor bleached by the sun's consuming light. That is why I like so much to wear it on my brow and on my clothing and have named it the color of truth.

3. Das Liedchen von der Ruhe (The Little Song About Repose; text by Ueltzen)

1. Good repose is found in the arms of love, but also in the bosom of the earth. Whether it is to be there, in the future, or here that I am to find repose, that I am to find repose: that is what my mind is investigating, and meditating and thinking and beseeching Providence, which grants it (repose), and beseeching Providence, which grants it.

2. Good repose is found in the arms of love, but alas! it beckons me in vain. With you, Elise, I would probably find the repose of my life, the repose of my life. The decision of cruel people keeps you from me, and I wither while in flower, I wither while in flower!

3. Good repose is found in the bosom of the earth, so quiet and undisturbed; here one's heart is so ridden with cares, there it is not burdened with anything, there it is not burdened with anything. One sleeps so softly, sleeps so sweetly to awaken in Paradise, to awaken in Paradise.

4. Ah, where will I one day find repose from all my burdens? Good repose is found in the arms of love, but also in the bosom of the earth; but also in the bosom of the earth! Soon I must rest, and where it is to be, the weary man no longer cares, the weary man no longer cares.

4. Mailied (May Song; text by Goethe)

How splendidly Nature is glowing before me, how the sun shines, how the meadow smiles! Blossoms are bursting out of every branch and a thousand voices out of the bushes, and joy and rapture out of every breast: O earth, O sun, O happiness, O pleasure! O love, O love! as beautiful and golden as the morning clouds on those heights! You give a splendid blessing to the fresh fields, to the whole world in its vapor of blossom. Oh, my girl, my girl, how I love you! What looks you give me! How you love me! As much as the lark loves song and the sky, and morning flowers love the fragrance of heaven, that is how I love you ardently, you that give me youth and joy and encouragement for new songs and dances. Be eternally happy in loving me, be eternally happy in loving me, be eternally happy in loving me!

5. Mollys Abschied (Molly's Departure; text by Bürger)

1. Farewell, man of pleasure and sorrows, man of love, prop of my life! God be with you, beloved, may my cry of blessing resound deep in your heart!

2. As a remembrance I offer you, not gold—what is gold and mercenary frippery?—rather I offer you all that your eyes found lovely in Molly, all that your heart found lovable in her.

3. Of my face, where you bestowed your kisses, take, for the duration of my absence from you, at least half, in the form of a silhouette, as a copy to enliven your imagination!

4. Take, sweet flatterer, some of my tresses, which you often entangled and disarrayed when you extolled them beyond the flax on Pallas' distaff, beyond gold and silk!

5. Let the memento of my eyes be this blue garland of supplicatory forget-me-nots, often sprinkled with the dew of mel-

ancholy that rises from the heart and bursts forth from them!

6. Lied (Song; text by Lessing)

1. Let the man who can do so live without love; even if he still remained a human being, he would not remain a man, he would not remain a man.

2. Sweet love, make my life sweet; lull to rest my excitable impulses without hindrance, without hindrance.

3. Let it be the duty of beautiful women to make us languish; but to make us languish forever—let it not be that, let it not be that.

7. Marmotte (Marmot; text by Goethe, partly in French [youngsters from the impoverished region of Savoie, exhibiting these ground squirrels from their native mountains, were part of the Parisian street scene])

I have now traveled through many lands *with my marmot,* and have always found something to eat, *with my marmot, with "si," with "la," with my marmot, with "si," with "la," with my marmot.* ["Si"and "la" may refer to the French names of the notes B and A.]

8. Das Blümchen Wunderhold (The Flower Wondrous-Fair; text by Bürger)

1. A little flower blooms somewhere in a quiet valley; it delights people's eyes and hearts as happily as the rays of the setting sun. It is much more precious than gold, than pearls or diamonds. Therefore it is very properly called the flower wondrous-fair.

2. A long song could surely be sung about the power of my little flower, about its great and miraculous effect on both body and spirit. That which no secret elixir can accomplish for you—in faith! my little flower will do for you, even though its appearance belies the fact.

3. Whoever keeps wondrous-fair in his bosom, becomes as lovely as an angel. This, with deep emotion, I have observed in both men and women. For both men and women, old or young, it acts as a talisman to attract irresistibly the homage of the most beautiful souls.

4. Ah, if you had only known the woman who was once my jewel—death tore her from my hand behind the very marriage altar!—then you would understand completely the power of wondrous-fair and you would gaze into the light of truth as if gazing at daylight.

Sechs Gesänge (Six Songs)

1. Mignon (text by Goethe, from Wilhelm Meisters Lehrjahre)

Do you know the land where the lemon trees bloom, where the golden oranges gleam in the dark foliage, where a gentle breeze blows from the blue sky, where the myrtle stands silently and the laurel grows tall? Do you know it? There, there is where I would like to go with you, my beloved; there, there is where I would like to go with you, my beloved, there, there!

Do you know the house? Its roof rests on columns, the great hall shines, the rooms glisten, and marble statues stand and look at me: "What have they done to you, you poor child?" Do you know it? There, there is where I would like to go with you, my protector, there, there is where I would like to go with you, my protector, there, there!

Do you know the mountain and its path among the clouds? The mule seeks its way among the mists; the ancient brood of the dragons dwells in caves; the crag drops away and the cataract tumbles over it. Do you know it? There, there is where our path leads! Oh, father, let us depart! There, there is where our path leads! Oh, father, let us depart! There, let us depart!

2. Neue Liebe, neues Leben (New Love, New Life; text by Goethe)

Heart, my heart, what is going on? What is troubling you so? What a strange new life! I no longer recognize you. Gone is all that you used to love, gone are those things that made you sad, gone are your diligence and your repose—ah, how did this happen to you? Are you bound with infinite strength by her bloom of youth, by her beautiful form, by her eyes full of fidelity and kindness? When I try to escape from her quickly, to take hold of myself, to run away from her, my path, alas, leads me back to her at the same moment, to her, my path leads back to her. Heart, my heart, what is going on? Heart, my heart, what is going on? What is troubling you so? What a strange new life! I no longer recognize you. Gone is all that you used to love, gone are those things that made you sad, gone is your repose—ah, how did this happen to you? How did this happen to you? Are you bound with infinite strength by her bloom of youth, by her beautiful form, by her eyes full of fidelity and kindness? When I try to escape from her quickly, to take hold of myself, to turn away from her, my path, alas, leads me back to her at the same moment, my path leads me back to her, to her at the same moment. And by this magic thread that cannot be torn the darling capricious girl keeps me bound in this way against my will; I must live within her magic circle in the way she wants. The change—oh, how great! Love! Love! let me go, let me, let me, let me go! let me, let me go!

3. Aus Goethe's Faust (From Goethe's Faust)

There was once a king who had a big flea, which he loved not a little, just as if it were his own son. So he called his tailor, the tailor arrived: "There, measure the squire for clothes and measure him for trousers!" Now he was dressed in velvet and silk, had ribbons on his robe, also had a cross (decoration) on it, and at once he was a minister and had a big star, and his brothers became great lords at court, too. And the court gentlemen and ladies were extremely tormented; the queen and her maid were bitten and gnawed, but were not allowed to crush them or scratch them away. But *we* can crush and smother them at once when one bites. CHORUS: But *we* can crush and smother them at once when one bites. Yes, *we* can crush and smother them at once, at once when one bites; yes, yes, *we* can crush and smother them at once when one bites, when one bites.

4. Gretels Warnung (Gretel's Warning; text by Halem)

1. Young, handsome Chris wooed with loving glances, playing of instruments and singing; no young man in the vicinity was so amiable, lively and slender. No, there was not one among their number who made me feel that way. He observed that, alas! and did not slacken until he obtained everything, everything, everything.

2. There was probably many a man in the village as young and handsome as he, but the girls looked at no one but him and flirted with him. Soon their flattering words stole him away; his heart was won. He became cold to me; soon afterwards he ran off and left me here, and left me here, and left me here in sorrow.

3. His loving glances, playing of instruments and singing, so sweet and blissful, his kiss that penetrated the soul, no longer delight me. See my case, all you sisters whom that perfidious man is now ardently courting, and do not believe what he says. Oh, look at me, poor me, oh, look at me and escape him.

5. An den fernen Geliebten (To Her Absent Lover; text by Reissig)

1. Once sweet repose and golden peace dwelt in my breast;

now, alas! since we have parted, melancholy is mingled with every pleasure.

2. I constantly hear the hour of separation resounding so muffled and hollow; in the evening song of the nightingales I can hear your farewell!

3. Wherever I go your lovely image floats before my eyes, filling my bosom with anxious yearning and rapture.

4. May your beautiful soul constantly be beseechingly reminded of what love says; O friend whom I have chosen from among the whole world, do not forget me!

5. When a breeze gently ruffles your hair in the moonlight, that is my spirit beseechingly murmuring around you: "Do not forget me!"

6. If in the light of the full moon you will long for me, like the sighing of the zephyr, you will hear, melodically sounding in the air: "Goodbye!"

6. Der Zufriedene (The Contented Man; text by Reissig)

1. To be sure, fortune made me neither rich nor great in this world, but I am as contented as if I had the finest lot, as if I had the finest lot.

2. A friend was granted me so much after my heart, for kissing, drinking, joking is his element, too, is his element, too.

3. With him many a bottle is emptied with gladness and wisdom, for on life's journey wine is the best horse, wine is the best horse.

4. If, enjoying this lot, a sadder one now befalls me, I think: no rose blooms without thorns in the world, blooms without thorns in the world.

Vier Arietten und ein Duett
(Four Ariettas and a Duet; Italian and German texts)

1. Hoffnung (Hope)

ITALIAN: My darling, tell me you love me, tell me you are mine, and I do not envy the gods their divine power! With a single glance of your eyes, dear woman, with a smile you open before me the paradise of my happiness, of my happiness, yes, of my happiness! Tell me, tell me, tell me you love me, my darling, tell me you love me, tell me you are mine; with a single glance of your eyes, dear woman, dear woman, with a smile you open before me the paradise of my happiness! With a single glance of your eyes, dear woman, dear woman, with a smile you open before me the paradise of my happiness, yes, of my happiness!

GERMAN: The gods are never eternally angry with the heart that loves; and in their hands sorrow is quickly turned into happiness! Boldly strive toward your goal! Live loyal to your hopes, and out of the storms will break the sweet light of fulfillment, yes, out of the storms will break the sweet light of fulfillment! Never, the gods are never angry, the gods are never eternally angry with the heart that loves; and in their hands sorrow is quickly turned into happiness, and quickly, and in their hands sorrow is quickly turned into happiness! Boldly strive toward your goal; live loyal to your hopes, to your hopes, and out of the storms will break the sweet light of fulfillment, the sweet light of fulfillment!

2. Liebes-Klage (Lament of Love; Italian text by Metastasio)

ITALIAN: Yes, I hear you, my heart, beating so wildly! I know that you want to complain, that you are in love, that you are in love. Ah! be silent about your pain; ah! suffer your torment. Be silent about it, be silent about it and do not betray my emotions, my emotions! Yes, I hear you, my heart, beating so wildly; ah! be silent about your pain; ah! suffer your torment. Be silent about it, be silent about it and do not betray my emotions, my emotions, be silent about it, be silent about it!

GERMAN: Only to the mute rocks do I lament about that which stirs my heart with deep pain, the anxious yearning, the source of my tears! Ah! she remains mute and distant; ah! she does not hear my sorrows! Merely in vain do I pour out bitter complaints of my melancholy from a full heart! Only to the mute rocks do I lament about that which, alas! stirs my heart with deep pain; ah! she remains silent and distant. Merely in vain do I pour out bitter complaints of my melancholy from a full heart, merely in vain, merely in vain!

3. L'amante impaziente/Stille Frage/Arietta buffa (The Impatient Lover/Silent Question/Comical Arietta; Italian text by Metastasio)

ITALIAN: What is my sweetheart doing, what is he [she?] doing? Why, why doesn't he come? He wants to see me languishing like this, like this, like this! Oh, how slowly the sun runs its course! Every moment seems like a day to me, every moment seems like a day to me, yes, yes, seems like a day to me! seems like a day to me! Ah! what is my sweetheart doing, what is he doing? Why, why doesn't he come? He wants to see me languishing like this, like this, like this! He wants to see me languishing like this, like this, like this! Why, why doesn't my sweetheart come? He wants to see me languishing, languishing like this! Why, ah! why doesn't my sweetheart come? He wants to see me languishing, languishing, languishing like this, like this, yes, see me languishing like this, like this, like this!

GERMAN: Will I never be allowed to approach you? Never receive a greeting from you, and read my destiny in your heavenly eyes? Are you angry at the audacious man? Are your eyes downcast in tenderness, in tenderness? Gods, change her stubborn mind! Grant me the long-desired happiness! Grant me happiness! Tell me, will I never be allowed to approach you? Never receive a greeting from you, and read my destiny in your heavenly eyes, and read my destiny in your heavenly eyes? Ah! are you, are you angry at the audacious man; your eyes, your eyes turn toward me tenderly! Ah! are you, are you angry at the audacious man; your eyes, your eyes, turn toward me in friendship, in friendship! Ah, are they, ah, are they, are your eyes turning tenderly, turning tenderly?

4. L'amante impaziente/Liebes-Ungeduld/Arietta assai seriosa (The Impatient Lover/Impatience of Love/Highly Serious Arietta)

ITALIAN: [Same text as foregoing.]

GERMAN: And so I must renounce it, the hope I nourished so long, and the laments of my yearning die quietly away in sorrow! Will you never return to me, heavenly hours that, alas! vanished too soon, never return to me, never return? How blissful I felt! How the moments, the moments, frolicked lightly and merrily around me! Will you never return to me, heavenly hours that alas, vanished too soon, heavenly hours, never return to me, never return, return? And so I must, and so I must renounce it, the hope I nourished so long, and the laments of my yearning die quietly away in sorrow! No, never, blissful hours, you will never return, never return, return, never return!

5. Lebens-Genuss. Duett (Enjoyment of Life. Duet; Italian text by Metastasio)

ITALIAN: *Soprano:* Listen to the breeze that softly sighs as it stirs the leaves and passes on; if you understand it, if you understand it, it speaks to you of love, yes, it speaks to you of love. *Tenor:* Listen to the stream that noisily wanders, while it groaningly pushes against its banks; if you understand it, if you understand it, it complains of love, yes, it complains of love. *Both:* Whoever feels that emotion in his heart knows by experience whether it is harmful or helpful, if it causes delight or pain! Whoever feels that emotion in his heart knows by experience whether it is harmful or helpful, if it causes delight or pain, delight or pain, or pain, delight or pain!

GERMAN: *Soprano:* Flowers that joy made into a garland for us fade quickly as the hours go by, and scarcely have we found happiness when it slips out of our hands, when it slips out of our hands! *Tenor:* But the darkness, too, which fate has given us, must pass away as the hours go by. Never resting, life speeds past; what is gone, never returns, never returns! *Both:* Oh, then let us firmly grasp present happiness by the golden edge of its garment, and enjoy ourselves as long as it tarries! Oh, then let us firmly grasp present happiness by the golden edge of its garment, and enjoy ourselves as long as it tarries, oh, as long as it tarries, it tarries, yes, as long as it tarries!

Drei Gesänge (Three Songs; texts by Goethe)

1. *Wonne der Wehmuth (Pleasure of Melancholy)*

Do not dry, do not dry, tears of eternal love! Do not dry! Ah, how dreary, how dead the world seems to eyes that are half-dry! Do not dry, do not dry, tears of unhappy love, of unhappy love! Do not dry, do not dry, tears of unhappy love, of unhappy love! Do not dry!

2. *Sehnsucht (Longing)*

What is tugging at my heart like this? What is dragging me outdoors, twisting and turning me out of my room and my house? How the clouds are sailing past the mountains there! I would like to cross them, I would like to travel there, I would like to travel there! Now the gregarious flight of the ravens rocks across the sky; I mingle among them and follow their procession. And we wave our pinions around hill and wall; she is dwelling down there, I search for her, I search for her. Here she comes walking; immediately I hasten to the bushy forest in the form of a songbird. She lingers and listens and smiles to herself: "He sings so beautifully and is singing to me, and is singing to me." The setting sun gilds the peaks; the beautiful woman, lost in thought, pays no attention. She follows the brook through the meadows, and her twisting path, her twisting path becomes dark and darker. All at once I appear in the form of a twinkling star. "What is shining up there, so near and so far?" And as soon as you have caught sight of its glow in amazement, I appear at your feet, and then I am happy, and then I am happy!

3. *Mit einem gemalten Band (With a Painted Ribbon)*

Kindly young gods of springtime, with a light hand and sportively, are strewing little flowers and little leaves for me upon an airy ribbon. Zephyr, take it on your wings, wrap it around my sweetheart's dress; and so she steps before her mirror in all her sprightliness. She sees herself surrounded by roses, herself like a young rose. [Grant me] one look, love of my life, and I am sufficiently rewarded. One look, love of my life, and I am sufficiently rewarded. Feel, feel what my heart is experiencing, hold out your hand to me freely, and let the bond that unites us not be a weak ribbon of roses, yes, let it not be a weak ribbon of roses! Feel what my heart is experiencing, hold out your hand to me freely, and let the bond that unites us not be a weak ribbon of roses, not be a weak ribbon of roses, no weak ribbon of roses!

Das Glück der Freundschaft/Lebensglück (The Joy of Friendship/Life's Joy; German and Italian texts anonymous)

GERMAN: That man lives a blissful life whose heart wins another heart; shared pleasure is doubled, shared sorrow vanishes. That man walks on flowery paths whom golden friend-ship lent its arm in intimate companionship in this brazen age. It [friendship] arouses our strength and spurs our courage for nothing but beautiful deeds, and nourishes within us the sacred ardor for truth and nature. That man has reached the goal of happiness who has found a female companion with whom the tender feelings of love have intimately linked him. Delighted by her, in her company, he finds his path beautified; through her alone the world blossoms for him and everything smiles upon him, everything, everything smiles upon him. That man lives a blissful life whose heart wins another heart; shared pleasure is doubled, shared sorrow vanishes, shared pleasure is doubled, shared sorrow, shared sorrow, shared sorrow vanishes.

ITALIAN: Happy is he who has been able to deserve faithful love! He will plow the sea of this life without fear. Wherever Heaven leads him, sweet flowers smile for him; joy is covered by no veil, sorrow is diminished. He feels his soul blaze with noble ardor; he is able to love truth alone, enjoy beauty only. Happy the man who can rest quietly on a faithful breast, and contentedly see his own image in his sweetheart's eyes. For even in the midst of disasters that sun will smile upon him, and everything will soon return to a lovelier tranquility, everything, everything will return. Happy is he who has been able to deserve faithful love! He will plow the sea of this life without fear, without fear, he will plow, he will plow the sea of this life, of this life.

An die Hoffnung
(To Hope; text by Tiedge, from *Urania*)

Is there a God? Will He one day fulfill what my longing weepingly promises itself? Will this mysterious Being reveal itself on some Judgment Day? Man must hope! He must not question! You that so gladly . . . [From this point on, the text, though with different repeats, is exactly the same as that of the first song in the present volume.]

An die ferne Geliebte
(To the Beloved Woman in Her Absence; song cycle with text by Jeitteles)

1. I sit on the hill peering out into the blue mist-laden land, searching for the far-off meadows where I met you, beloved. I am widely separated from you; mountains and valleys lie as a barrier between us and our peace, our happiness and our sorrow. Alas, you cannot see my glances hastening to you so ardently, and my sighs die away in the space that separates us. Will nothing, then, reach you any more? Will nothing be love's messenger? I will sing, sing songs that will complain to you of my grief! For all space and all time flee before the music of song, and a loving heart attains what a loving heart has consecrated!

2. Where the mountains so blue look down from the misty gray, where the sun ceases glowing, where the clouds cover the sky—that is where I would like to be, that is where I would like to be! There in the calm valley pains and sorrow are silent. There where the primrose quietly meditates among the rocks, where the wind blows so softly—that is where I would like to be, that is where I would like to be! Off to the contemplative forest I am urged by the force of love, by inner grief, by inner grief. Ah, I could not be drawn away from here, beloved, if I could be with you forever, be with you forever!

3. [You clouds] weightlessly sailing high above, and you small, narrow brook, if you can catch sight of my darling, bring her thousands of greetings from me. If you clouds then see her walking, lost in thought, in the quiet valley, let my image arise before her in the airy hall of heaven. If she then stands by the bushes, which are now yellowed and stripped

by autumn, complain to her of what has become of me, complain to her, birds, of my sorrow! Soft west winds, in your blowing deliver to my heart's choice my sighs, which perish like the last ray of the sun. Whisper my supplication of love to her, small and narrow brook, let her see faithfully reflected in your waters my tears without number, without number!

4. These clouds high above, the merry procession of these songbirds will see you, graceful woman. Take me along in your airy flight! These west winds will play and sport around your cheeks and breast, will ruffle your silken tresses. If I could share this pleasure with all of you! This little brook busily hastens toward you from those hills. If her image is reflected in you, then flow back without delay, then flow back without delay, yes, without delay!

5. Springtime is returning, the meadow is in blossom. The breezes are blowing so gently and warmly; the brooks are now running with such a chattering. The swallow returns to the hospitable roof, it builds its bridal chamber so diligently; love is to dwell in it, love is to dwell in it. It busily brings from all around many a soft bit for the nuptial bed, many a warm bit for its young. Now the wedded pair live together so faithfully; those that winter separated, the spring has now united; it knows how to join those who love; it knows how to join those who love. Springtime is returning, the meadow is in blossom. The breezes are blowing so gently and warmly. Only I cannot leave this place. When the spring joins all who love, only for our love does no spring appear, and tears are all that it acquires, and tears are all that it acquires, yes, all that it acquires.

6. Take them then, beloved, these songs I have sung to you; then sing them again in the evening to the sweet sound of the lute! When the red of sunset then moves toward the quiet blue lake and its last ray goes out behind that mountain peak, and you sing, and you sing what I sang, what rang out from the fullness of my heart without ostentation of art, with consciousness only of longing, with consciousness only, only of longing: then, in the face of these songs, all that has separated us so widely will yield, and a loving heart will attain what a loving heart has consecrated, and a loving heart will attain what a loving, a loving, a loving heart consecrated! Then, then, in the face of these songs, all that has separated us so widely will yield, and a loving heart will attain what a loving heart, a loving heart consecrated, what, what a loving, loving heart consecrated!

Der Mann von Wort
(The Man of His Word; text by Kleinschmid)

1. You said, friend, "I will return to this place"; those were your words. You did not come; is that a man on whose word one can rely, on whose word one can rely?

2. I can hardly imagine anything greater than to be the man of one's word; someone who breaks his word, as women do, does not deserve the name of man, does not deserve the name of man.

3. "I'll keep my word" was a German saying that went from the lips to the heart, and the clasp of German hands bound it fast like sacred oaths, bound it fast like sacred oaths.

4. And this word that he gave to you was not broken by fear in the proximity of the grave, not by a woman's favor, nor by human pressures, not by gold, not by property, nor by princely rank, not by gold, not by property, nor by princely rank.

5. If your German ancestor spoke thus, then, as a son, follow in the steps of your father, who as a man of his word can guarantee his oath, "I'll keep my word," can guarantee it as a man of his word.

6. Now we also are worthy of the Germans, that people which the world honors. Here is my hand; let us shake hands upon it and be true German men, and be true German men.

Merkenstein (for two voices; text by Rupprecht)

1. Merkenstein! Merkenstein! Wherever I go, I think of you. When dawn reddens the mountains, the blackbird sings brightly in the bushes and flocks scatter as they graze, I think about you, Merkenstein!

2. Merkenstein! Merkenstein! In the sultry suffering of noon I long for your walks, your grottoes, your cliffs, to enjoy your coolness. Merkenstein! Merkenstein!

3. Merkenstein! Merkenstein! The evening star's glow illuminates you for me; I see your rooms shining and fragrant with Flora's garlands all around; the moon peeps in companionably. Merkenstein! Merkenstein!

4. Merkenstein! Merkenstein! Night envelops me for you alone. I would like to dream rapturously forever beneath your sister trees, and to grant myself your peace! Merkenstein! Merkenstein!

5. Merkenstein! Merkenstein! Let the morning be stimulating; from the knightly peaks there let us seek for the images of the past: they so great, and we so small! Merkenstein! Merkenstein!

6. Merkenstein! Merkenstein! Most graceful association of pleasures! In you, Nature appeared to me eternally young in the midst of ruins; in order to dedicate myself constantly to her [Nature] and her only, I think of you, Merkenstein!

Der Kuss/Ariette
(The Kiss/Arietta; text by Weisse)

I was all alone with Chloe and wanted to kiss her, and I wanted to kiss, kiss, kiss her: but she said that she would scream, she would scream, she would scream, she would scream; that it was lost labor, lost labor, that it was lost, lost labor. I risked it anyway, and kissed her, and kissed her in spite of her resistance, in spite of her resistance. And didn't she scream? O, yes, she screamed, she screamed; but, but, but much later, but, yes but, but much later, she screamed, but much, much, much, much, much, much, much, much, much later, later, yes, much, much later.

Schilderung eines Mädchens
(Description of a Girl; text anonymous)

Friend, do you want me to describe Elise? May the spirit of [the painter Johann Leonard] Uz flow into me! As stars beam on a winter night [Friedrich Ludwig] Oeser would paint the splendor of her eyes.

An einen Säugling
(To an Infant; text by Wirths
[?; or by J. von Döhring?])

You still don't know whose child you are, who gives you your diapers, who watches over you, or who she is that warms and nurses you.

Meanwhile, enjoy yourself with a pious mind, enjoy yourself! In a few years the woman who cares for you will be revealed to be your mother.

Thus all of us here are protected and cared for in a similarly unknown way by a Donor—may He have thanks for it!—of possessions, drink and food.

To be sure, my clouded mind cannot fathom Him, but in a few years, if I remain pious and believing, He will reveal Himself to me.

Abschiedsgesang an Wien's Bürger beim Auszug der Wiener Freiwilligen
(Song of Farewell to the Citizens of Vienna on the Marching Out of the Viennese Volunteers; text by Friedelberg)

1. No lament is to resound when the banner leaves here; tears are to fall from no eyes that follow it as it goes. It is pride in this ornament and a feeling of civic dignity that glow on every face, that glow on every face. It is pride in this ornament and a feeling of civic dignity that glow on every face, that glow on every face.

2. Friends, wish us luck on our noble journey in triumphant tones. Beautiful women, let your soulful glances follow us cheerfully. To augment our country's glory we set out courageously and will return to you more worthy, and will return to you more worthy. To augment our country's glory we set out courageously and will return to you more worthy, and will return to you more worthy.

3. Even a villain, perhaps, can stand defiantly in front of the [cannon's] thundering maw. To unite a gentle mind with courage, to honor humanity—that he cannot do. Never to disturb the happiness of the virtuous, to love one's countrymen fraternally: that is the duty of German heroes, that is the duty of German heroes! Never to disturb the happiness of the virtuous, to love one's countrymen fraternally: that is the duty of German heroes, that is the duty of German heroes!

4. Rejoice, fathers; exult, mothers! Nowhere that our corps appears, not even amid the enemy, will it elicit bitter tears from innocence. We wish to avenge ourselves nobly, to be silent until our deeds speak for us; let the enemy himself admire them, let the enemy himself admire them! We wish to avenge ourselves nobly, to be silent until our deeds speak; let the enemy himself admire them, let the enemy himself admire them!

5. [You will find us] better human beings, better citizens than when we left; you will see no immoral killers in us when we return. Our Vienna will receive us again wreathed with glory, strong and honest. Onward, let the banner wave aloft! Onward, let the banner wave aloft! Our Vienna will receive us again wreathed with glory, strong and honest. Onward, let the banner wave aloft! Onward, let the banner wave aloft!

6. Let us follow this banner enriched by [Maria] Theresa's artistry; let its gold band remind us: "May virtue make us equal to princes." Ha! when we bring it back, we will sing jubilantly: "This [gold] band held Austria, this band held Austria!" Ha! when we bring it back, we will sing jubilantly: "This band held Austria, this band held Austria!"

Krieglied der Oesterreicher
(War Song of the Austrians; text by Friedelberg)

1. We are a great German nation; we are powerful and just. You Franks (French), do you doubt it? You Franks do not know us well. For our prince is good, our courage is high! Sweet is the blood of our grapes, and beautiful our women; how could things be better for us, how could things be better for us? CHORUS: How could things be better for us, how could things be better for us?

2. We do not fight for glory or pay, only for the happiness of peace! We return, poor in others' gold, to our hearth. For only for good citizens does the blessing of nature bloom on vineyard, forest and field. Our war is a just one; the victory belongs to us, to us, the victory belongs to us, to us. CHORUS: The victory belongs to us, to us, the victory belongs to us.

3. With pikes, scythes and guns, hasten here, both small and great! For the fatherland! Small and great, sound, sound the battle cry! Here we stand immovable for our homes, farms and country, with weapons in our hands, and we join battle valiantly, no matter how many enemies there are, no matter how many enemies there are! CHORUS: No matter how many enemies there are, no matter how many enemies there are!

4. Man, woman and child in Austria have a deep sense of their own worth. Never, Franks, will we be defeated by you, never will we be deluded! For our prince is good, our courage is high! Sweet is the blood of our grapes, and beautiful our women; how could things be better for us, how could things be better for us? CHORUS: How could things be better for us, how could things be better for us?

Der freie Mann (The Free Man; text by Pfeffel)

1. CHORUS: Who, who is a free man? ONE VOICE: The man to whom only his own will, and not any whim of an overlord, can give laws; *he* is a free man! a free, free man! CHORUS: *He* is a free man! a free, free man!

2. Who is a free man? The man who respects the law, does nothing that it forbids, wants nothing that is not within his power and rights; *he* is a free man!

3. Who is a free man? The man for whom neither birth nor titles, neither velvet coat nor workman's smock can conceal the presence of a brother; *he* is a free man!

4. Who is a free man? The man who, secure within himself, can outface the venal favors of great and small; *he* is a free man!

5. Who is a free man? The man who, solidly grounded, can endure ingratitude, even when it comes from his fatherland; *he* is a free man!

6. Who is a free man? The man who, even when he must give up both his property and his life for liberty, nevertheless can lose nothing; *he* is a free man!

7. Who is a free man? The man who, when death summons him, can look boldly at the threshold of the grave and also backwards; *he* is a free man!

Opferlied (Song of Sacrifice; text by Matthisson)

1. The flame blazes up, a gentle glow shines through the gloomy oak grove, and the fragrance of incense wells up, and the fragrance of incense wells up. Oh, lend a gracious, a gracious ear to me; and let the young man's sacrifice be acceptable to you, O most high, acceptable to you, O most high!

2. Be always the defense and shield of liberty! May your spirit of life gently breathe through air, earth, fire and waters, air, earth, fire and waters! Give me, as a young man, as a young man and as an old man, at my ancestral hearth, O Zeus, O Zeus, the beautiful together with the good, the beautiful together with the good.

Der Wachtelschlag (The Quail's Cry; text by Sauter)

Listen, how the sound comes so sweetly from there! "Fear God! Fear God!" the quail calls in my ear. Seated outdoors, surrounded by stalks, the listener by the grainfield is reminded: "Love God! Love God! He is so kind and gentle, He is so kind, so kind and gentle." Once more its jerky call signifies: "Praise God! Praise God, Who is able to reward you. Do you see the splendid fruits of the field? Take it to heart, inhabitant of the world! Thank God! Thank God, Who feeds and sustains you, Who feeds and sustains you." When the Lord of nature frightens you in the storm, and the quail calls: "Implore God! Implore God!," He spares the fields. When dangers from enemies make you fearful—"Trust in God! Trust in God!," and lo! He does not tarry long. When the Lord of nature frightens you in the storm, implore God! Implore God! When dangers from enemies make you fearful, trust in God! Trust in God, and lo! He does not tarry long, lo! He does not tarry, does not tarry long. Implore God! Trust in God! Trust in God! Lo! He does not tarry, does not tarry long.

Als die Geliebte sich trennen wollte/
Empfindungen bei Lydiens Untreue
(When His Loved One Wanted to Leave Him/
Feelings About Lydia's Faithlessness;
text by Breuning after the French of Soulié)

The last glimmer of hope is fading away; she has broken all her oaths with her volatile temperament; so, as a consolation, let me also lose forever the consciousness, the consciousness that I was too happy! What have I said? No, no decision, no power can rescue me from these chains of mine; alas! at the very brink of despair the memory remains eternally, eternally sweet to me! Ha! dear hope, return to me, stir up all my flames with one look, no matter how great the pains of love may be; the man who loves, the man who loves never finds his lot altogether unhappy! And you that reward faithful love with vexation, do not fear the breast in which your image still dwells; this feeling heart could never hate you; forget? forget?—it will sooner succumb to its sorrow, it will sooner succumb to its, its sorrow.

Lied aus der Ferne
(Song from Far Away; text by Reissig)

When my tears of longing were not yet flowing, and distant parts were not yet enviously keeping my sweetheart from me, how my life then resembled a blossoming garland, a nightingale grove, full of games and full of dancing, full of games and full of dancing! How my live then resembled a nightingale grove, full of games and full of dancing, yes, full of games and full of dancing, full of games and full of dancing! Now longing often drives me out to the mountaintops, to try to see the wish of my heart smiling somewhere! My languishing gaze seeks her in this vicinity, but it returns, never satisfied. What a beating there is in my breast, as if you were near me; oh, come, my loved one, your young lover is here! I sacrifice to you all that God has lent me, for I have never yet loved as much as I love you, for I have never yet loved as much as I love you, for I have never yet loved as much as I love you, yes, I have never yet loved as much as I love you, never yet, never yet! O dear one, come quickly to the nuptial dance! I am already nurturing roses and myrtles for the wreath. Come, come quickly, I am already nurturing roses and myrtles for the wreath. Come, magically transform my cottage into the temple of peace, the temple of bliss, and you be the goddess! Come, transform my cottage into the temple of peace, the temple of bliss, and you be the goddess, you be the goddess! Come, transform my cottage into the temple of bliss, and you be the goddess, yes, you be the goddess! You be the goddess, yes, you be the goddess!

Der Jüngling in der Fremde
(The Young Man in Distant Parts; text by Reissig)

1. Springtime blossoms forth from the womb of nature; with smiling flowers it strews the fields: but valley and hilltop smile in vain for me; such feelings of anxiety and sorrow remain in my heart.

2. Inspiriting springtime, you do not heal my pain! Life has crushed my happy heart. Ah, if repose possibly still blooms on earth for me, then lead me to the lap of that celestial one (Repose)!

3. I sought her (Repose) in the morning in the blossoming valley; here the brooks danced in the purple beams, and love sang flatteringly in the fragrant greenery, but I did not see smiling Repose blooming there.

4. Then I sought her at noon, stretched out on flowers, covered with the shade of falling petals; a cooling breeze played about my face, but I did not see flattering Repose here.

5. Now I sought her in the evening in the lonesome grove; the nightingale poured its song into the silence, and the moon shone through the roof of foliage so beautifully, but I did not see my Repose here either!

6. Ah, heart, this young man does not recognize you any more; how sad you are; what is paining you so? You are tortured by longing, just admit that to me, you are bound by the girl from our native fields!

Der Liebende
(The Man in Love; text by Reissig)

1. What a strange feeling of life, a mixture of pain and pleasure, what a trembling such as I have never felt before holds sway now in my breast, holds sway now in my breast! Heart, my heart, what does this beating mean? Your peace is interrupted; tell me, what has happened to you? I have never seen you like this, I have never seen you like this, I have never seen you like this!

2. Hasn't the divine flower inflamed you with the breath of love, the flower that blossomed in the shrine of pure innocence, blossomed in the shrine of pure innocence? Yes, the beautiful heavenly blossom, with the enchanting eyes full of kindness, holds me fast with bonds that cannot be torn apart, that cannot be torn apart, that cannot be torn apart.

3. Often I try to escape from the dear one; then tears tremble in my eyes, and the spirits of love draw me back at once, draw me back at once. For this heart always beats longingly for her with ardent pounding, but alas! she does not feel my heart's message expressed in my eyes, my heart's message expressed in my eyes, my heart's message expressed in my eyes.

Sehnsucht (Longing; text by Reissig)

The quiet night spreads its refreshing darkness over valley and hilltop; the star of love twinkles, gently welling up in the lake. In the branches, nature's songsters have fallen mute; a mysterious silence rests upon the flowery fields. Ah, my weary eyes alone are not closed in slumber: come, relieve my agitation, you silent god of rest! Gently dry my tears, make room for sweet joy; come, kindly deceive my longing with a blissful dream! Oh, conjure up before my eyes my sweetheart who evades me; let me press her to my heart, so that noble love is ignited! You sweetheart whom I have in mind, how I long for you; appear, ah, appear and give me hope with your smile!

Des Krieger's Abschied
(The Warrior's Departure; text by Reissig)

1. I leave for the battle aflame with love, but I depart without tears; my arm belongs to the fatherland, my heart to my beautiful beloved; for the true hero must constantly feel a tender love for a girl, and yet be able to die in battle resolutely for the fatherland!

2. I have never fought in order to obtain a decoration as a prize; O Love, I have wanted to receive one from your hands alone; let a German maiden's hand crown my victorious life, my arm belongs to the fatherland, my heart to my beautiful beloved!

3. When in the battle, warmed by love, I think about my beloved back home, then I would like any one to try to resist this arm; for—what a reward!—my darling's hand will crown my victorious life; my arm belongs to the fatherland, my heart to my beautiful beloved!

4. Farewell, my darling, honor and duty now summon the German warriors; farewell, farewell and do not cry; I will return home victorious; and if I fall by the enemy's hand, then my fame will still resound: my arm belongs to the fatherland, my heart to my beautiful beloved!

Der Bardengeist
(The Bard's Spirit; text by Herrmann)

1. There on the high cliff sang an ancient bard's spirit; it sounded like the music of an aeolian harp in a fearful, heavy dirge that tore my heart to shreds.

2. And as the sacred Castalian spring flowed gently and mildly from the mountain down to the sweet flowery plain, so did his silvery garment wave and flap in the morning wind.

3. His song poured out very softly in the gray glow of twilight, and his heart and deep thoughts floated up to the bright stars in sweet daydreams.

4. And his strange song gripped me silently more and more. What do you see, spirit so fearful and heavy? What do you seek there in the host of stars? How your soul struggles!

5. "I am seeking, it is true, but, alas! I no longer find, the past. I see, it is true, so fearfully and heavily, I seek there in the host of stars, the golden age of the Germans.

6. "The sun has already set; hardly an afterglow has remained; with malice and with impudent scorn dreary night now plants the poppy (of oblivion) around the grave of our fathers.

7. "Yes, noble, unshaken, bold the German once stood here; alas! fateful stars travel past over frail ruins. Teutonia is no more."

8. The ancient bard's spirit was still singing on the high cliff; sounding like the music of an aeolian harp came a fearful, heavy dirge that tore my heart to shreds.

Ruf vom Berge
(The Call from the Mountain; text by Treitschke)

1. If I were a little bird, and also had two little wings, I would fly to you! But because that may not be, I remain here.

2. If I were a little star, and also had many beams, I would beam on you. And you would look up in a friendly way, and send up your greetings.

3. If I were a little brook, and also had many waves, I would noisily rush through the greenery. When I came near your little foot, I would kiss it.

4. If I became an evening breeze, I would take the fragrance of blossoms, and breathe it on you. Lingering on your breast and lips, I would find repose there.

5. For no hour of the night passes when my heart does not awaken and think of you, and how you have given me your heart a thousand times.

6. Of course, brook and star, little breeze and little bird travel far and arrive where you are. Only I am forced to remain here and weep.

An die Geliebte
(To the Loved Woman, text by Stoll; two different settings)

Oh, let me drink from your cheek the tear shed by your placid eyes in their lovable shining before the earth swallows it up! It is lingering on your cheek and ardently wishes to devote itself to fidelity; now that I receive it this way in a kiss, now your sorrows are also mine, now, now your sorrows are also mine, now, now your sorrows are also mine, mine, mine!

So oder so (This Way or That; text by Lappe)

1. North or south! As long as a shrine of beauty and the Muses, a heaven rich in gods, blooms in one's warm bosom! The winter can kill only spiritual poverty: the north adds strength to strength and glow to glow. North or south! As long as the soul is ardent!

2. City or countryside! Just let the space not be too confined; a little sky, some green in the trees as shade from the burning sun. Blissfulness is not tied to any specific place; who has ever found happiness outside himself? City or countryside! The external world is frippery!

3. Poor or rich! Be it peach or plum, we pick unequally from the tree of life; you take from the bough, I only from the branch. My meal, though light, is not trivial on that account; the pleasure received in their consumption determines the value of things. Poor or rich! The happy are rich!

4. Pale or ruddy! Only on pale cheeks are found longing and love, anger and fear, sympathy and consolation for the distress of others. The spirit does not shine forth from the pool of blood; a different mirror burns in the brightness of the sun. Pale or ruddy! As long as the eyes are not lifeless!

5. Young or old! What do we care about the years? The spirit is fresh, but the hair has a (silvery) shine; *my* hair, too, is graying too soon! But go on, my tresses, hasten to take on that gleaming color; there is no harm in acquiring silver. Young or old! But not cold until the grave!

6. Sleep or death! Welcome, twin brothers! The day is over; you close our eyelids. Earthly happiness and distress are a dream. Too short the day! Life passes too soon! Why is it so beautiful and yet floats away so quickly? Sleep or death! Brightly shines the dawn!

Das Geheimniss
(The Secret; text by Wessenberg)

Where does the flower bloom that never fades? Where does the star shine that glows eternally? Let your lips, O Muse, let your sacred lips tell me about that flower and that star, tell me about that flower and that star. "My lips cannot inform you of it, unless your own inner being tells you. Deep inside you you will find that glowing and that blooming; happy is each man who watches over them faithfully! Happy is each man who watches over them faithfully! Deep inside you you will find that glowing and that blooming; happy is each man who watches over them faithfully!"

Resignation (text by Haugwitz)

Go out, go out, my light! What you are lacking is now gone, in this place you cannot find it again! You must now detach yourself, yes, you must now detach yourself. In the past you flared up merrily, now your air has been snatched away; when this (air) has blown away, the flame wanders aimlessly— seeks—seeks—does not find— go out, my light! Go out, go out, go out, my light! What you are lacking is now gone, in this place you cannot find it again; you must now detach yourself. Go out, go out, go out, my light!

Abendlied unter'm gestirnten Himmel
(Evening Song Under the Starry Sky; text by Goeble)

When the sun sinks down, and the day inclines toward rest; when the moon beckons silently in a friendly way and night descends; when the stars glitter splendidly and a thousand Milky Ways glimmer: the soul feels so great and wrests itself out of the dust. It gazes so gladly at those stars, as if looking back at its homeland; it gazes up at those bright distant places and forgets earth's frippery; it desires only to struggle, it desires only to strive, to soar up out of its shell: the earth is too narrow and small for it, it wants to be among the stars. Even if storms rage on earth, and false happiness rewards the evil man, it (the soul) looks hopefully upward where the Judge of stars sits enthroned. No fear can torture it any more, no power can give it orders; with transfigured countenance it flies up to the heavenly light. A quiet premonition comes tremblingly over me from those worlds; my earthly pilgrimage will not last long, not long any more; soon I shall have attained my goal, soon I shall have soared up to you, soon I shall reap at God's throne the beautiful recompense for my sorrows, yes, soon, soon, the beautiful recompense for my sorrows.

Andenken (Remembrance; text by Matthisson)

I think of you when the harmonies of the nightingales echo through the grove! When do you think of me? When, when do you think of me? I think of you in the twilight glow of evening by the shady fountain! Where do you think of me? Where, where do you think of me? I think of you with sweet sorrow, with anxious longing and hot tears! How do you think of me? How, how do you think of me? Oh, think, oh, think of me, oh, think of me until we are rejoined on a better planet! However far away, I think of you alone, I think of you alone! Oh, think, oh, think of me, oh, think of me, until we are rejoined on a better planet! However far away, I think of you alone, I think of you alone, I think of you alone, you alone, you alone, you alone, you alone, yes, you alone, you alone!

Ich liebe dich (I Love You; text by Herrosee)

I love you as you love me, in the evening and in the morning; there has never yet been a day on which you and I have not shared our cares. Also, when shared they were easy for you and me to bear; you consoled me when I had anxieties, and I wept when you lamented, when you lamented. And so, God's blessing on you, you joy of my life; may God protect you and keep you for me, and keep us both; may God protect you, keep you for me, protect and keep us both, keep, keep us both, keep us both.

Sehnsucht
(Longing; text by Goethe
from *Wilhelm Meisters Lehrjahre*;
four consecutive settings)

1. Only the person accustomed to longing knows how I am suffering! Alone and cut off from all joy, I look up at the sky in that direction yonder.

2. Ah! the man who loves me and knows me is far away. My head spins, I am on fire inside. Only the person accustomed to longing knows how I am suffering!

La partenza/Der Abschied
(The Departure; Italian text by Metastasio
with anonymous German translation)

ITALIAN: Here is that cruel moment! Nice, my Nice, farewell! How will I live, my darling, so far from you? I will live in constant sorrow, I will have no more pleasure, and you—who knows if you will ever remember me? And you—who knows if you will ever remember me?

GERMAN: This is the fearful hour; ha! my lips are trembling; poor me, how can I live far from you, O Nice? I must live in sorrow; without you joys flee; and you, will you too grant me a loving thought when far away? And you, will you too grant me a loving thought when far away?

In questa tomba oscura
(In This Dark Tomb; Italian text by Carpani
with anonymous German translation)

ITALIAN: In this dark tomb let me rest; while I lived, ungrateful woman, you should have thought of me, thought of me. Let the naked ghosts enjoy peace at least, and do not, and do not moisten my ashes with needless poison. In this, in this dark tomb let me rest; while I lived, ungrateful woman, you should have thought of me, thought of me, ungrateful woman, ungrateful woman!

GERMAN: Now that I have died, let me alone in the darkness of this grave; yes, while I lived, faithless woman, ah! you should have thought of me, thought of me! Oh, let my heart rest in peace among the naked ghosts, and do not weepingly moisten my ashes with vain, vain sorrow. In this, in this dark grave let me alone now that I have died; while I was on earth, false woman, oh, did you then think of me? of me? of me? you faithless, false heart!

Seufzer eines Ungeliebten/und/Gegenliebe
(Sighs of an Unloved Man/and/Reciprocated Love;
texts by Bürger)

Have you not allotted love to the life of every creature? Why am I alone forgotten—you too, my mother! you, Nature? Where might there live in forest or sheepfold, or where in sky or sea, an animal that was never loved, that was never loved? Everything is loved, everything except me, except me, yes, everything except me! Even though in the grove, in the fields and mountain meadows, trees and bushes, mosses and herbs form pairs through love and reciprocated love, no woman becomes my partner, no woman. Even though in the grove, in the fields and mountain meadows, trees and bushes, mosses and herbs form pairs through love and reciprocated love, no woman becomes my partner, no woman. Honeyed fruit never ripens into pleasure for me from the sweetest of urges. For, alas! I lack the reciprocated love that one woman, only one woman can supply; for, alas! I lack the reciprocated love that only one woman can supply, can supply.

If I knew, if I knew, if I knew that you cared for me and valued me a little, and felt only a hundredth part of what I feel for you; (if I knew) that your thanks would prettily meet my greeting halfway and your lips would gladly give and take again an exchanged kiss: then, O heaven, my heart, beside itself, would completely go up in flame! I would not be able to let you demand my body or my life in vain! Reciprocated favor heightens favor, love is nourished by reciprocated love, and that which would have remained a tiny spark amid the ashes flares up into a blazing fire, and that which would have remained a tiny spark amid the ashes flares up into a blazing fire. If I knew, if I knew, if I knew, if I knew that you cared for me and valued me a little, and felt only a hundredth part of what I feel for you; that your thanks would prettily meet my greeting halfway and your lips would gladly give and take again an exchanged kiss: then, O heaven, my heart, beside itself, would completely go up in flame! I would not be able to let you demand my body or my life in vain! Reciprocated favor heightens favor, love is nourished by reciprocated love, and that which would have remained a tiny spark amid the ashes flares up into a blazing fire, and that which would have remained a tiny spark among the ashes flares up into a blazing fire; that which would have remained a tiny spark among the ashes, that which would have remained a tiny spark among the ashes.

Die laute Klage
(The Loud Lament; text by Herder)

Turtledove, you lament so loudly and rob this poor man of his only solace, the sweet sleep of oblivion: turtledove, I mourn like you, and hide my mourning deep in my wounded heart, in my locked breast. Ah, love makes a cruel distribution! It gave you the loud lament of mourning as a consolation, as a consolation—to me, taciturn sorrow! Ah, love makes a cruel distribution! It gave you the loud lament of mourning as a consolation, as a consolation—to me, taciturn sorrow, to me, to me, taciturn sorrow!

AN DIE HOFFNUNG

(aus Tiedges Urania)

in Musik gesetzt von

L. van BEETHOVEN.

Op.32.

Singstimme.

PIANOFORTE.

Poco adagio.

Die du so
Wenn, längst ver_
Und blickt er

gern in heil'gen Näch_ten fei_erst, und sanft und weich den Gram ver_schleierst, der ei_ne zar_te
hallt, ge_lieb_te Stim_men schweigen; wenn un_ter aus_ge_storb_nen Zwei_gen ver_ö_det die Er_
auf, das Schicksal an _ zu _ kla_gen, wenn scheidend ü_ber sei _ nen Ta_gen die letz_ten Strah _ len

See _ le quält, o Hoff _ nung! lass, durch
inn_rung sitzt: dann na _ he dich, wo
un _ ter _ gehn: dann lass ihn, um den

dich em_por ge_ho_ben, den Dul_der ah _ nen, dass dort o_ben ein En_gel
dein Ver_lass_ner trau_ert, und, von der Mit _ ter_nacht um_schau_ert, sich auf ver
Rand des Er_den_trau_mes, das Leuchten ei _ nes Wol_ken_sau_mes, von ei_ner

sei _ ne Thrä _ nen zählt! O Hoff _ nung! lass, durch
sunk _ ne Ur _ nen stützt. Dann na _ he dich, wo
na _ hen Son _ ne, sehn! Dann lass ihn, um den

dich em_por ge_ho_ben, den Dul_der ah _ nen, dass dort o_ben ein En_gel
dein Ver_lass_ner trau_ert, und, von der Mit _ ter_nacht um_schau_ert, sich auf ver
Rand des Er_den_trau_mes, das Leuchten ei _ nes Wol_ken_sau_mes, von ei_ner

sei _ ne Thrä _ nen zählt!
sunk _ ne Ur _ nen stützt.
na _ hen So _ ne, sehn!

ADELAIDE

(Gedicht von Matthisson)

in Musik gesetzt von

L. van BEETHOVEN.

Op.46.

Ein-sam wan — delt dein Freund im Frühlings — gar-ten, mild vom lieb-lichen Zauberlicht um—

flos-sen, das durch wan — kende Blü-thenzwei-ge zittert, A — dela—

i — de! A — dela — i — de! In der spie-gelnden Fluth, im

Schnee der Al_pen, in des sin_ken_den Ta_ges Goldge_wöl_ke, im Ge_fil _ de der

Ster_ne strahlt dein Bild_niss, dein Bild_niss, A _ de _ la _ i _ de!

in des sin_ken_den Tages Goldge_wöl_ke, im Ge_fil _ de der Ster _ ne

strahlt____ dein Bildniss, dein Bildniss, A _ _ de_la _ i _ de!

A _ bend _ lüft _ chen im zarten Laube

A _ de _ la _ i _ de!   A _ de _ la _ i _ de!

Allegro molto.

Einst, o Wunder! o Wunder! ent _ blüht, auf mei _ nem Gra _ be,

o Wunder! ent _ blüht, auf mei _ nem Gra _ be, ei _ ne Blu _ me der

A _ sche meines Her _ zens, der _____ A _ sche mei _ nes Herzens; deut _ lich

schimmert, deut _ lich schimmert auf je _ dem Purpur _ blättchen, auf je _ dem Purpur _ blättchen:

SECHS LIEDER VON GELLERT

in Musik gesetzt von

L. van BEETHOVEN.

Dem Grafen Browne gewidmet.

Op. 48.

N.º 1. Bitten.

Feierlich und mit Andacht.

Gott, dei_ne Gü_te reicht so weit, so weit die Wol_ken ge_hen; du krönst uns mit Barm_her_zig_keit, und eilst, uns bei_zu_ste_hen. Herr! mei_ne Burg, mein Fels, mein Hort, ver_nimm mein Flehn, merk auf mein Wort; denn ich will vor dir be_ten! denn ich will vor dir be_ten!

Original_Verleger: Artaria & C.º in Wien.

Nº 2. Die Liebe des Nächsten.

Lebhaft doch nicht zu sehr.

Singstimme.

PIANOFORTE.

So Jemand spricht: Ich lie_be Gott! und hasst doch seine Brüder, der

treibt mit Got_tes Wahr _ heit Spott, und reisst sie ganz dar _ nieder. Gott

ist die Lieb', und will, dass ich den Nächsten lie _ be, gleich als mich.

Nº 3. Vom Tode.

Mässig und eher langsam als geschwind.

Singstimme.

PIANOFORTE.

Mei_ne Lebens_zeit ver_streicht, stündlich eil' ich zu dem Gra_be,

und was ist's, das ich viel _ leicht, das ich noch zu le_ben ha_be?

Denk', o Mensch, an dei_nen Tod! Säu_me nicht, denn Eins ist Noth. Säu_me

nicht, _____ denn Eins ist Noth. Säu_me nicht, _____ denn Eins ist

Noth.

Nº 4. Die Ehre Gottes aus der Natur.

Die Himmel rühmen des Ewigen Ehre, ihr Schall pflanzt seinen Namen fort. Ihn rühmt der Erdkreis, ihn preisen die Meere; vernimm, o Mensch, ihr göttlich Wort!

Wer trägt der Himmel unzählbare Sterne? Wer führt die Sonn' aus ihrem Zelt? Sie kömmt und leuchtet und lacht uns von ferne, und läuft den Weg, gleich als ein Held, und läuft den Weg, gleich als ein Held.

No 5. Gottes Macht und Vorsehung.

Gott ist mein Lied! Er ist der Gott der Stär_ke;

hehr ist sein Nam' und gross sind sei_ne Wer_ke, und al_ _ le Him_mel

sein Ge _ biet.

N.º 6. Busslied.

An dir al_lein, an dir hab' ich ge _ sün_digt, und ü _ bel oft vor dir ge_

than. Du siehst die Schuld, die mir den Fluch ver _ kündigt; sieh, Gott, auch meinen Jammer, meinen

Jam _ _ mer an. Dir ist mein Flehn, mein

Seuf _ zen nicht ver _ bor_gen, und mei _ _ ne Thrä _ _ nen sind vor dir. Ach

Gott, mein Gott, wie lan_ge soll ich sor_gen? wie lang' entfernst du dich von mir? Herr,

hand_le nicht mit mir nach mei_nen Sünden, ver_gilt mir nicht, ver_gilt mir nicht nach

mei _ ner, nach mei _ _ ner Schuld. Ich su_che dich; lass mich dein Antlitz

finden, du Gott der Langmuth und Ge _ duld, der Langmuth und Ge _ duld.

Attacca subito.

Allegro ma non troppo.
(Geschwind doch nicht zu viel.)

Früh wollst du mich mit dei_ner Gnade fül_len, Gott,

Va_ter der Barm_her_zig_keit. Er_freu_e mich um

deines Na_mens wil_len; du bist ein Gott, der gern er_freut.

Lass dei_nen Weg mich wie_der freu_dig

wal - len, und leh - re mich dein hei - lig

Recht, dein hei-lig Recht, mich täg-lich thun nach dei-nem Wohl - ge -

fal - len; du bist mein Gott, ich bin dein

Knecht. Herr, ei - le du, mein

Schutz, mir bei-zu-ste - hen, und lei - te mich auf

ACHT GESÄNGE UND LIEDER
in Musik gesetzt von
L. van BEETHOVEN.
Op.52.

No 1. Urians Reise um die Welt.
(Claudius.)

In einer mässigen geschwinden Bewegung mit einer komischen Art gesungen.

Singstimme.

1. Wenn jemand eine Reise thut, so kann er was ver_zählen. Drum nahm ich meinen Stock und Hut und

PIANOFORTE.

thät das Reisen wählen. Da hat er gar nicht übel d'ran gethan, verzähl' er doch weiter, Herr U _ ri _ an!

2.
Zuerst ging's an den Nordpol hin;
Da war es kalt, bei Ehre!
Da dacht ich denn in meinem Sinn,
Dass es hier besser wäre.
Tutti.
Da hat er gar nicht übel d'ran gethan,
Verzähl' er doch weiter, Herr Urian!

5.
Nun war ich in Amerika!
Da sagt'ich zu mir: Lieber!
Nordwestpassage ist doch da:
Mach' dich einmal darüber!
Chor wie zuvor.

8.
Allein, allein, allein, allein,
Wie kann ein Mensch sich trügen!
Ich fand da nichts als Sand und Stein,
Und liess den Sack da liegen.
Chor wie zuvor.

3.
In Grönland freuten sie sich sehr,
Mich ihres Orts zu sehen,
Und setzten mir den Thrankrug her:
Ich liess ihn aber stehen.
Tutti.
Da hat er gar nicht übel d'ran gethan,
Verzähl' er doch weiter, Herr Urian!

6.
Flugs ich an Bord und aus in's Meer,
Den Tubus festgebunden,
Und suchte sie die Kreuz und Quer,
Und hab'sie nicht gefunden.
Chor wie zuvor.

9.
D'rauf kauft'ich etwas kalte Kost
Und Kieler Sprott und Kuchen,
Und setzte mich auf Extrapost,
Land Asia zu besuchen.
Chor wie zuvor.

4.
Die Esquimeaux sind wild und gross,
Zu allem Guten träge:
Da schalt ich Einen einen Kloss
Und kriegte viele Schläge.
Tutti.
Da hat er gar nicht übel d'ran gethan,
Verzähl' er doch weiter, Herr Urian!

7.
Von hier ging ich nach Mexico;
Ist weiter als nach Bremen,
Da, dacht'ich, liegt das Gold wie Stroh;
Du sollst 'n Sack voll nehmen.
Chor wie zuvor.

10.
Der Mogul ist ein grosser Mann
Und gnädig über Massen,
Und klug; er war itzt eben dran,
'n Zahn ausziehn zu lassen.
Chor wie zuvor.

11.
Hm! dacht ich, der hat Zähnepein,
Bei aller Gröss' und Gaben!—
Was hilft's denn auch noch: Mogul sein?
Die kann man so wohl haben.
Chor wie zuvor.

13.
Nach Java und nach Otaheit,
Und Afrika nicht minder;
Und sah'bei der Gelegenheit
Viel Städt'und Menschenkinder.
Tutti.
Da hat er gar nicht übel d'ran gethan,
Verzähl' er doch weiter, Herr Urian!

12.
Ich gab dem Wirth mein Ehrenwort,
Ihn nächstens zu bezahlen;
Und damit reist'ich weiter fort
Nach China und Bengalen.
Chor wie zuvor.

14.
Und fand es überall wie hier,
Fand überall 'n Sparren,
Die Menschen grade so wie wir,
Und eben solche Narren.
Tutti.
Da hat er übel, übel d'ran gethan;
Verzähl'er nicht weiter, Herr Urian!

N° 2. Feuerfarb'.

(Sophie Mereau.)

weiss ei_ne Far_be, der bin ich so hold, die ach_te ich hö_her als Sil_ber und Gold; die
Bläu_e des Himmels strahlt herr_lich und mild, d'rum gab man der Treu_e dies freundli_che Bild. Doch
rum ich, so fragt ihr, der Far_be so hold den hei_li_gen Na_men der Wahrheit ge_zollt? weil

trag' ich so ger_ne um Stirn und Ge_wand, und ha_be sie Far_be der Wahrheit genannt.
trü_bet manch Wölkchen den Ae_ther so rein! so schleichen beim Treu_en oft Sor_gen sich ein.
flam_men_der Schimmer von ihr sich er_giesst, und ru_hi_ge Dau_er sie schützend umschliesst.

2. Wohl blü_het in lieb_li_cher, sanf_ter Ge_stalt die
4. Die Far_be des Schnees,___ so strah_lend und licht, heisst
6. Ihr scha_det der nas_sen_de Re_gen_guss nicht, noch

calando *a tempo*

glü_hen_de Ro_se, doch blei_chet sie bald. D'rum weih_te zur Blu_me der
Far_be der Un_schuld; doch dau_ert sie nicht. Bald ist es ver_dun_kelt das
bleicht sie der Son_ne ver_ _zeh_ren_des Licht, d'rum trag' ich so gern sie um

calando *a tempo*

Lie_be man sie; ihr Reiz ist un_end_lich, doch wel_ket er früh.
blen_den_de Kleid: so trü_ben auch Un_schuld Ver_ leum_dung und Neid.
Stirn und Ge_wand und ha_be sie Far_be der Wahr_heit ge_nannt.

p

№ 3. Das Liedchen von der Ruhe.

(H.W.F. Ueltzen.)

Adagio.

Singstimme.

PIANOFORTE.

1. Im Arm der Lie_be ruht sich's wohl, wohl auch im Schooss der Er_de. Ob's dort noch o_der hier sein soll, wo Ruh' ich fin_den wer_de, wo Ruh' ich fin_den wer_de, das forscht mein Geist, und sinnt und denkt und fleht zur Vor_sicht, die sie schenkt, und fleht zur Vor_sicht, die sie schenkt.

Nº 4. Mailied.

(Goethe.)

Wie herrlich leuch_tet mir die Na_tur, wie glänzt die Sonne, wie lacht die Flur! Es drin_gen Blüthen aus je _ dem Zweig und tau_send Stim_men aus dem Ge_sträuch, und Freud'und Wonne aus je _ der Brust: o Erd', o Son_ne, o Glück, o Lust!

Lieb', o Lie_be! so gol_den schön, wie Mor_gen_wolken auf je_nen Höhn! du seg_nest herrlich das fri_sche Feld, im Blü_then_dam_pfe die vol_le Welt. O Mäd_chen, Mädchen, wie lieb' ich dich! wie blickt dein Au_ge, wie liebst du mich!

So liebt die Ler_che Ge _ sang und Luft, und

Mor_gen_blumen den Him_mels_duft, wie ich dich lie _ be mit war _ mem Blut, die

du mir Ju_gend und Freud'und Muth zu neu_en Liedern und Tän_zen giebst. Sei e _ wig

glück_lich,wie du mich liebst, sei e _ wig glücklich,wie du mich liebst, sei e _ wig

glücklich,wie du mich liebst!

Nº 5. Mollys Abschied.

(Bürger.)

Adagio con espressione.

Singstimme.

1. Le _ be wohl, du Mann der Lust und Schmer_zen, Mann der
2. Zum Ge _ dächt _ niss biet' ich dir, statt Gol_des _ was ist
3. :Vom. Ge _ sicht, der Wahl_statt dei _ ner Küs _ se, nimm, so
4. Nimm, du süs _ ser Schmeichler,von den Lo_cken, die du
5. Mei _ ner Au _ gen Denkmal sei dies blau _ e Kränz_chen

PIANOFORTE.

Lie _ be, mei_nes Le_bens Stab! Gott mit dir, Ge _ lieb_ter, tief zu Herzen hal_le dir mein
Gold und gol_des_wer_ther Tand? _biet' ich lie_ber, was dein Au _ ge hol_des,was dein Herz an
lang' ich .fer_ne von dir bin, ..halb zum Min_de _ sten .im Schatten _ ris_se für die Fan_ta_
oft zer_wühltest und ver _ schobst,wann du ü _ ber Flachs an Pal _ las Ro_cken, ü _ ber Gold und
fle _ hen_der Ver_gissmein_nicht, oft be_träu_felt von der Weh_muth Thaue, der her_vor durch

Se _ gens_ruf hin _ ab!
Mol _ ly Lie_bes fand.
sie die Abschrift hin!
Sei _ de sie er _ hobst!
sie vom Her_zen bricht!

Nº 6. Lied.

(Lessing.)

1. Oh _ ne Lie _ be le _ be, wer da kann; wenn er auch ein
2. Sü _ sse Lie _ be, mach' mein Le _ ben süss; stil _ le ein die
3. Schmachten las _ sen sei der Schö _ nen Pflicht; nur uns e _ wig

Mensch schon blie _ be, bleibt er doch kein Mann, bleibt_____ er doch kein
re _ gen Trie _ be son _ der Hin _ der _ niss, son _ _ der Hin _ der
schmach _ ten las _ sen, die _ ses sei sie nicht, die _ _ ses sei sie

Mann.
niss.
nicht.

Nº 7. Marmotte.

Ich kom _ me schon durch man _ ches Land, a _ vec que la mar _
mot _ te, und im _ mer was zu es _ sen fand, a _ vec que la mar _ mot _ te, a _
vec que si, a _ vec que la, a _ vec que la mar _ mot _ te, a _ vec que si, a _ vec que la, a _
vec que la marmot _ te.

№ 8 . Das Blümchen Wunderhold.

(Bürger.)

1. Es blüht ein Blümchen irgendwo in einem stillen Thal, das schmeichelt Aug' und Herz so froh wie Abend-Sonnenstrahl. Das ist viel köstlicher als Gold, als Perl' und Diamant. Drum wird es Blümchen Wunderhold mit gutem Fug genannt.

2. Wohl sänge sich ein langes Lied von meines Blümchens Kraft, wie es am Leib' und am Gemüth so hohe Wunder schafft. Was kein geheimes Elixir dir sonst gewähren kann, das leistet, traun! mein Blümchen dir, man säh' es ihm nicht an.

3. Wer Wunderhold im Busen hegt, wird wie ein Engel schön. Das hab' ich, inniglich bewegt, an Mann und Weib gesehn. An Mann und Weib, alt oder jung, zieht's, wie ein Talisman, der schönsten Seelen Huldigung unwiderstehlich an.

4. Ach, hättest du nur die gekannt, die einst mein Kleinod war, der Tod entriss sie meiner Hand hart hinter'm Traualtar! dann würdest du es ganz verstehn, was Wunderhold vermag, und in das Licht der Wahrheit sehn wie in den hellen Tag.

SECHS GESÄNGE

in Musik gesetzt von

L. van BEETHOVEN.

Der Fürstin von Kinsky gewidmet.

Op. 75.

No 1. Mignon.

(Goethe.)

Kennst du das Land, wo die Ci-tro-nen blühn, im dunkeln Laub die Gold-O-ran-gen glühn, ein sanf-ter Wind vom blau-en Him-mel weht, die Myr-the still und hoch der Lor-beer steht? Kennst du es wohl?

Höh _ _ len wohnt der Dra _ chen al _ te Brut; es stürzt der

Fels und ü _ ber ihn ____ die Fluth.

Kennst du ihn wohl? Da _ hin! ___ da _ hin ___ geht un_ser Weg! o Va _ ter,

lass uns zieh'n! Da _ hin! da _ hin geht un_ser Weg! o Va _ ter, lass uns

zieh'n! Da _ hin lass ____ uns ziehn!

Nº 2. Neue Liebe, neues Leben.

Herz, mein Herz, was soll das ge_ben? was be_drän_get dich so sehr? welch ein

frem_des neu_es Le_ben! ich er_ken_ne dich nicht mehr. Weg ist al_les was du lieb_test, weg wa_

rum du dich be_trübtest, weg dein Fleiss und dei_ne Ruh'_

ach, wie kamst du nur da_zu! wie kamst du nur da_zu!

Fes_selt dich die Ju_gend_blü_the, die_se

lieb_li_che Ge_stalt, die _ _ser Blick voll Treu' und Gü_te mit un_end_li_cher Ge_

walt? Will ich raschmichihrent_zie_hen, mich er_mannen, ihr ent_flie_hen, führet

mich im Au_gen_blick, ach, mein Weg zu ihr zu_rück, zu ihr, _____ zu ihr mein

Weg zu_rück. Herz, mein Herz, was soll das ge_ben? _____ Herz, mein

Herz, was soll das ge_ben? was be_dränget dich so sehr? welch ein fremdes neues Le_ben! ich er_ken_nedichnicht

mehr. Weg ist al_les was du lieb_test, weg wa_rum du dich be_trüb_test, weg dein Fleiss und deine

Ruh'___

Langsam

ach wie kamst du nur da_zu! wie kamst du nur da_

Im vorigen Zeitmaasse.

zu!

Fesselt dich die Jugend_blüthe,

diese

lieb_li_che Ge_stalt, die_ _ _ser Blick voll Treu' und Gü_te mit un_end_li_cher Ge_

walt?_____

Will ich rasch mich ihr ent_ziehen, mich er_mannen, ihr ent_flie_hen, führet

mich im Augen_blick, ach, mein Weg zu ihr zu_rück, führet mich im Au_gen_blick zu

ihr, _____ zu ihr mein Weg zu_rück. Und an diesem Zauber_fädchen, das sich

nicht zerreissen lässt, hält das lie_be lo_se Mädchen mich so wi_der Willen fest; muss in ih_rem Zauber_

krei_se le_ben nun auf ih_re Wei _ se. Die Ver_ändrung, ach, wie gross! Liebe! Lie_be! lass mich los! lass,

lass, lass mich los! lass, lass _____ mich los!

Nº 3. Aus Goethe's Faust.

In

cresc.

p

Sammet und in Sei_de war er nun an_ge_than, hat_te Bänder auf dem Kleide, hatt' auch ein Kreuz da_

ran, und war sogleich Mi_ni_ster, und hatt' einen grossen Stern, da wurden seine Ge_schwister bei

Hof' auch grosse Herr'n.

Und Herr'n und Frau'n am Hofe, die wa_ren sehr ge_

plagt, die Kö_ni gin und die Zo_fe ge_stochen und ge_nagt, und durften sie nicht knicken, und

weg sie jucken nicht. Wir knicken und er_sticken doch, doch gleich, wenn ei_ner sticht. Wir knicken und er_

Chor.

sti - cken doch, doch gleich, wenn ei_ner sticht. Ja, wir knicken und er_sticken doch gleich, gleich, wenn ei_ner

sticht, ja, ja, wir kni_cken und er_sti_cken doch, doch gleich, wenn ei_ner sticht, wenn ei_ner

sticht.

Nº 4. Gretels Warnung.

Singstimme.

PIANOFORTE.

Etwas lebhaft mit leidenschaftlicher Empfindung, doch nicht zu geschwind.

1. Mit Lie_bes_blick und Spiel und Sang, warb Chri_stel jung und schön, so
2. Wohl war im Dor_fe man_cher Mann, so jung und schön wie er; doch
3. Sein Lie_bes_blick und Spiel und Sang, so süss und won_nig_lich, sein

lieb_lich war so frisch und schlank kein Jüng_ling rings zu sehn. Nein, kei_ner war in ih_rer Schaar, für
sahn nur ihn die Mäd_chen an und ko_sten um ihn her, bald riss ihr Wort ihn schmeichelnd fort; ge_
Kuss, der tief zur See_le drang, er_freut nicht für_der mich. Schaut meinen Fall, ihr Schwestern all, für

den ich das ge_fühlt. Das merkt' er, ach! und liess nicht nach, bis er es all, bis
won_nen war sein Herz. Mir ward er kalt, dann floh er bald und liess mich hier, und
die der Fal_sche glüht, und trau_et nicht dem was er spricht. O seht mich an, mich

er es all, bis er es all er_hielt.
liess mich hier, und liess mich hier im Schmerz.
Ar_me an, o seht mich an, und flieht.

1.2. | 3.

№ 5. An den fernen Geliebten.

(Chr. L. Reissig.)

Singstimme

Larghetto.

1. Einst wohn_ten sü_sse Ruh und gold__ner
2. Der Tren_nung Stun_de hör' ich im__mer
3. Wo_hin ich wand_le schwebt vor mei__nen
4. Stets mahn' es fle__hend dei__ne schö__ne
5. Wenn sanft ein Lüft__chen dei_ne Lo__cken
6. Wirst du im Voll__mond_schein dich nach mir

PIANOFORTE.

Frie_den in mei_ner Brust, nun mischt sich Weh_muth ach! seit wir ge_
hal_len so dumpf und hohl, mir tönt im A_bend_lied der Nach_ti_
Bli_cken dein hol_des Bild, das mir mit ban_ger Sehn_sucht und Ent_
See_le, was Lie_be spricht, ach Freund! den ich aus ei__ner Welt er_
kräu_selt im Mon_den_licht, das ist mein Geist, der fle_hend dich um_
seh_nen, wie Ze_phyrs Weh'n, wird dir's me_lo_disch durch die Lüf_te

schie_den, in je_de Lust.
gal_len dein Le_be_wohl!
zü_cken den Bu_sen füllt.
wäh_le, ver_giss mein nicht!
säu_selt, ver_giss mein nicht!
tö_nen, auf Wie_der_sehn!

No. 6. Der Zufriedene.

(Chr. L. Reissig.)

Froh und heiter, etwas lebhaft.

Singstimme.

PIANOFORTE.

1. Zwar schuf das Glück hie _ nie _ den mich
   ganz nach mei _ nem Her _ zen ward
   ihm wird froh und wei _ se manch
   mir bei die _ sem Loo _ se nun

we _ der reich noch gross,
mir ein Freund ver _ gönnt,
Fläschchen aus _ ge _ leert !
auch ein trüb'res fällt ;

al _ lein ich bin zu _ frie _ den, wie mit dem schönsten
denn küs _ sen, trinken, scherzen, ist auch sein E _ le
denn auf der Le _ bens _ rei _ se ist Wein das be _ ste
so denk'ich, keine Ro _ se blüht dornlos in der

Loos, wie mit dem schönsten Loos.
ment, ist auch sein E _ le _ ment.
Pferd, ist Wein das be _ ste Pferd.
Welt, blüht dorn _ los in der Welt.

1.2.3. | **4.**

2. So
3. Mit
4. Wenn

VIER ARIETTEN UND EIN DUETT

(Italienisch mit deutscher Uebersetzung)

in Musik gesetzt von

L. van BEETHOVEN.

Op.82.

Nᵒ 1. Hoffnung.

Dimmi, ben mi _ o, che m'a _ mi, dim_mi che mi_a tu se_i,

Nimmer dem lie_benden Her _ zen zürnen auf e_wig die Götter;

e non in_vi_dio ai Dei ___ la lor' di_vi___ni_tà! Con un tuo sguardo

und schnell in ih_rer Hand ___ wird Leid in Glück ___ ge_wandt! Kühn nur zum Ziele

so_lo, ca_ra, con un sor_ri_so tu m'apri il pa_ra_

streben! Treu nur der Hoff_nung le_ben, und aus den Stür__men

di _ so di mia fe_li_ci _ tà, di mia fe_li_ci _ tà, sì, di mia fe_li_ci_
bricht der Gewührung sü_sses Licht, ja, aus den Stürmen bricht der Ge_währung sü_sses

tà! Dimmi, dimmi, dimmi che m'a _ _
Licht! Nimmer, nimmer zürnendie Göt _ _

_ _ _ _ mi, dim_mi, ben mi_o, che m'a_mi, dim_mi che mi _ a tu
_ _ _ _ ter, nimmerdem lie_ben_den Her _ zen zürnen auf e _ wig die

se _ _ i; con un tuo sguar _ do so _ lo, ca _ ra, ca_ra, con un sor_
Göt _ _ ter, und schnell in ih _ rer Hand wird Leid in Glück _ _ ge_wandt, und

Nº 2. Liebes-Klage.

Singstimme.

Adagio ma non troppo.

T'in _ ten _ do, sì, mio cor, con
Den stummen Fel_sen nur klag'

PIANOFORTE.

pp

tan_to pal _ pi _ tar! So ___ che ti vuoi la _ gnar, che a _ man _ _ te
ich, was mir das Herz be _ wegt mit tie _ fem Schmerz, das ban _ ge

tr   tr

se _ i, che a _ man _ _ te se _ i. Ah! taci il tu _ o do _
Sehnen, die Quel _ le mei _ ner Thränen! Ach! sie bleibt stumm und

cresc.   p   tr   p

lor, ah! soffri il tuo mar _ tir. ___ Ta _ ci _ lo, ta _ ci _ lo e non tra _
fern, ach! sie hört nicht mei _ ne Lei _ den! Nur umsonst ström' ___ ich meiner

f   p   cresc.

Nº 3. L'amante impaziente.

Stille Frage.

Nº 4. L'amante impaziente.

Liebes-Ungeduld.

Arietta assai seriosa.

Andante con espressione.

Nᵒ 5. Lebens-Genuss.

DREI GESÄNGE

(Gedichte von Goethe)

in Musik gesetzt von

L. van BEETHOVEN.

Der Fürstin von Kinsky gewidmet.

Op. 83.

Nº 1. Wonne der Wehmuth.

Andante espressivo.

Componirt im Jahre 1810.

Singstimme.

PIANOFORTE.

Trocknet nicht, trocknet nicht, Thrä_nen der e_wi_gen Lie _ be! Trocknet nicht! Ach nur dem halb_ge_trock_ne_ten Au_ge wie ö_de, wie todt die Welt ihm er_scheint! Trock_net nicht,

ritard.

trock_net nicht, Thrä_nen un_glück_li_cher Lie_be, un_glück_li_cher Lie _ _ be!

cresc. *sf* *sf* *ritard.*

a tempo

Trock_net nicht, trock_net nicht, Thrä_ _ nen un _ glück_li_cher Lie_ _be!

a tempo *cresc.* *f* *dim.* *p* *f*

un _ glück _ li _ cher Lie _ be! Trock_net nicht!

dim. *p*

Nº 2. Sehnsucht.

wiegt sich der Ra_ben ge _ sel_li _ ger Flug; ich mi_sche mich drunter und fol_ge dem Zug. Und

non ligato
fz

ritard. - - - - - a

Berg und Ge_mäu_er um _ fit _ ti _ gen wir; sie wei_let da drun_ten,ich spä_he nach ihr, ich

p ritard. - - - - *p*

tempo

spä_he nach ihr.

Da

tempo
tr *tr*
cresc.
fp

kommt sie und wan_delt; ich ei _ le so_bald ein sin_gen_der Vo_gel zum bu_schi_gen Wald. Sie

pp

schlingt sich der Gang, um schlingt sich der Gang.

Auf

ein mal er schein' ich ein blin ken der Stern. „Was glän zet da dro ben, so

nah und so fern?" Und hast du mit Staunen das Leuchten er blickt; ich lieg dir zu Füssen, da

bin ich be glückt, da bin ich be glückt!

Nº 3. Mit einem gemalten Band.

Ze_phyr, nimm's auf dei_ne Flü_gel, schling's um mei_ner Liebsten

Kleid; und so tritt sie vor den Spie_gel all in ih_rer Mun_ter_

keit. Sieht mit Ro_sen sich um_ge_ben, selbst wie

ei_ne Ro_se jung. Ei_nen Blick, ge_lieb_tes Le_ben! und ich bin be_lohnt ge_

nung. Ei _ nen Blick, ge_lieb _ _tes Le_ben! und ich bin__ be_lohnt ge _

nung. Füh_le, füh _ le, was diess Herz em _

pfin _ det, rei _ che frei mir dei _ ne Hand,__ und das

Band, das uns ver_bin_det, sei kein schwa_ches Ro _ sen _

DAS GLÜCK DER FREUNDSCHAFT

(Lebensglück)

in Musik gesetzt von

L. van BEETHOVEN.

Op. 88.

Freundschaft gab in die_ser ehr_nen Zeit.
cuo_pre un vel, si sce_ma o_gni do _ lor.
Sie
Ei

weckt die Kraft und spornt den Muth zu schö_nen Tha_ten nur,_____ und nährt in uns die
sen_te l'ul_ma di_vam_par di ge_ne_ro so ar_dir;_____ il ve_ro ei puo_te

heil'_ge Glut für Wahr_heit und Na_tur. Er_rei_chet hat des Glü_ckes Ziel, wer
sol a_mar, del bel_lo sol gio_ir. Fe_li_ce chi ad un fi_do sen può

ei_ne Freun_din fand, mit der der Lie_be Zart_ge_fühl ihn
*che_to ri_po_sar, e negl' oc_chiet_ti del suo ben con_*

in_nig_lich ver_band. Ent_zückt von ihr, ihr bei_ge_sellt, ver_
ten_to si spec_chiar! *Che in mez_zo agli dis_a_stri an_cor quel*

schö_nert sich die Bahn; durch sie _____ al_lein blüht
sol gli ri_de_rà, ed a _____ più bel_la

ihm die Welt und Al_les lacht ihn an, Al_les,
cal_ma or or tut_to gli tor_ne_rà, tut_to,

Al_les, Al_les lacht ihn an. _____ Der
*tut_to, tut_to tor_ne_rà. _____ Be_*

AN DIE HOFFNUNG
(aus Tiedge's Urania)

in Musik gesetzt von

L. van BEETHOVEN.

Der Fürstin von Kinsky gewidmet.

Op. 94.

Larghetto.

Die du so gern in heil'gen Näch_ten fei_erst, und sanft und weich den Gram____ ver_schleierst, der ei_ne zar_te See_le quält,____ o Hoff _ nung! lass, durch dich empor ge _ ho_ben, den Dul _ _ der ah_nen, dass dort o _ _ ben ein En_gel sei_ne Thrä _ nen zählt! O Hoff _ nung, o

Hoff _ nung! lass, durch dich em _ por ge _ ho _ ben, den Dul _ der ah _ nen, dass dort o _ ben ein

En _ gel sei _ ne Thrä _ nen zählt, ein En _ gel sei _ ne Thrä _ nen zählt, ein En _ gel sei _ ne Thrä _ nen

zählt! Wenn, längst verhallt, ge _

lieb _ te Stimmen schweigen, wenn un _ ter aus _ gestorb'nen Zweigen ver _ ö _ det die Er _ inn'rung sitzt:

dann na_he dich, na_he dich, wo dein Ver_lass_ner trau_ert, und,

von der Mit_ter_nacht umschauert, sich auf ver_sunk_ne Ur_ _ nen stützt.

Und blickt er auf, das Schicksal an_zu_kla_gen, wenn scheidend ü_ber sei_nen

Adagio. **Tempo I.**

Ta_gen die letzten Strahlen un_ter _ gehn: dann lass ihn um den

Rand des Er_den_traumes das Leuchten ei_nes Wol_kensaumes von ei _ ner na _ hen Son _ ne

sehn, von ei _ ner na _ _ hen Son _ ne sehn! Die

du _ so gern,_ die du so gern in heil'gen Näch _ ten feierst, und sanft und weich den Gram _ ver_

schleierst, der ei_ne zar_te See_le quält,_ o Hoff _ nung! lass, durch dich empor ge_

ho_ben, den Dul _ _ der ah_nen, dass dort o _ _ ben ein En_gel sei_ne Thrä _ _ nen

zählt! O Hoff_nung, o Hoff_nung! lass, durch dich empor ge _ ho_ben, den Dul _ _ der

ah_nen, dass dort o _ _ ben ein En_gel sei_ne Thrä _ nen zählt, ein En_gel sei _ ne Thrä _ nen

zählt, ein En _ _ gel sei _ ne Thrä _ nen zählt!____   O Hoffnung!

AN DIE FERNE GELIEBTE

Ein Liederkreis von A. Jeitteles

in Musik gesetzt von

L. van BEETHOVEN.

Op.98.

№ 1.

Ziemlich langsam und mit Ausdruck.

Componirt im April 1816.

Ach, den Blick kannst du nicht se — hen, der zu dir so glü — hend

eilt, und die Seuf — zer, sie ver — we — hen in dem Rau — me, der uns

theilt. Will denn nichts mehr zu dir drin-gen, nichts der Lie-be Bo — te

sein? Sin-gen will ich, Lie-der sin-gen, die dir kla-gen mei-ne Pein!

Denn vor Lie — des-klang ent-wei — chet je-der Raum und je — de

Dort im ru_higen Thal schweigen Schmer_zen und Qual. Wo im Ge_stein still die

Pri_mel dort sinnt, weht so lei_se der Wind, möch_te ich sein! möch_te ich sein!

Nach und nach *stringendo*

geschwinder.

Ziemlich geschwind.
Assai allegro.

Hin zum sin_ni_gen Wald drängt mich Lie_bes_ge_

Poco adagio.   **Tempo I.**

walt, in_ne_re Pein, in_ne_re Pein. Ach, mich zög's___ nicht von

Poco adagio.

hier, könnt' ich, Trau_te, bei dir e_wig_lich sein! e_wiglich

lasst mein Bild vor ihr ent_ste_hen in dem luft'_gen Him_mels_saal.

Wird sie an den Bü_schen ste_hen,

die nun herbst_lich falb und kahl, klagt ihr, wie mir ist ge_sche_hen, klagt ihr, Vög_lein,

mei_ne Qual!

Stil_le We_ste, bringt im We_hen

Nº 4.

Nicht zu geschwinde, angenehm und mit viel Empfindung.

Die - se Wol - ken in den Hö - hen, die - ser Vög - lein munt' rer

Zug wer - den dich, o Hul - din, se - hen. — Nehmt mich mit im leichten Flug!

cresc. *cresc.* *f* *p* *f* *p*

Die - se We - ste wer - den spie - len scher - zend dir um Wang' und

Brust, in den seid' - nen Lo - cken wüh - len. — Theilt' ich mit euch die - se

sempre p *cresc.* *f* *p*

Lust! Hin zu dir von je - nen Hü - geln em - sig

f *p*

die _ ses Bäch_lein eilt. Wird ihr Bild sich in dir spie_geln, fliess zu_

cresc. cresc.

Nach und nach geschwinder.
Sempre più allegro.

rück dann un_ver_weilt! fliess zu _ rück dann un_ver_weilt, ja un_ver_weilt!

cresc.

Nº 5.

Vivace.   Poco adagio.   Tempo I.

Es keh_ret der Mai_en, es

blü_het die Au'. Die Lüf_te, sie we_hen so mil_de, so lau_ge_schwä_tzig die Bä_che nun rin _ _ nen.

Die Schwalbe, die keh_ret zum wirth_li_chen Dach, sie baut sich so em_sig ihr

bräut_lich Gemach, die Lie_be soll wohnen da drin _ nen, die Lie_be soll woh_nen da drin _ nen.

Sie bringt sich geschäf_tig von Kreuz und von Quer manch

weiche_res Stück zu dem Brautbett hie her, manch' wärmendes Stück für die Klei _ nen. Nun

wohnen die Gatten bei_sammen so treu, was Win_ter geschieden, ver_band nun der Mai, was lie_bet, das weiss er zu

ei _ nen, was lie _ bet, das weiss er zu ei _ nen.

Es kehret der Mai _ en, es blü _ het die Au'. Die Lüf _ te, sie we _ hen so mil _ de, so lau. Nur

ritard. — — — —   Tempo I.

ich kann nicht zie _ hen von hin _ nen.   Wenn Al _ les, was lie _ bet, der Frühling vereint, nur

ri — — — — tar — — — — dan —

un _ se _ rer Lie _ be kein Früh _ ling erscheint, und Thrä _ nen sind all ihr Ge _ win _ nen, und

— — — — do   Adagio.

Thränen sind all ihr Ge _ win _ nen,   ja, all ihr Ge _ win _ nen.

Nº 6.

Andante con moto, cantabile.

Nimm sie hin denn, die _ se Lie_der, die ich dir, Ge _ lieb_te, sang, sin _ ge sie dann A _ bends wie_der _ zu der Lau_te sü _ ssem Klang! Wenn das Dämm'rungs_roth dann zie_het nach dem stil _ len blau_en

ritard.

ritard.
dim.

DER MANN VON WORT

Gedicht von F. A. Kleinschmid
in Musik gesetzt von

L. van BEETHOVEN.

Op. 99.

Wor-te, gleich den Wei-bern, bricht, ver-dient des Man-nes Na-men nicht, ver - dient des Man-nes

Na-men nicht.

3. Ein Wort, ein Mann, war deut-scher Klang, der von dem Mund zum Her-zen drang, und

das der Schlag von deutscher Hand, gleich heil'gen Ei-den, fest ver-band, gleich heil'gen Ei-den,

fest ver-band.

4. Und die_ses Wort, das er dir gab, brach nicht die Furcht am na_hen Grab, nicht

Wei_bergunst, noch Menschenzwang, nicht Gold, nicht Gut, noch Fürstenrang, nicht Gold, nicht Gut, noch

Für_sten_rang.

5. Wenn so dein deut_scher Ah _ ne sprach, dann folg', als Sohn, dem Va _ ter nach,

der sei _ nen Eid: Ein Wort, ein Mann, als Mann von Wort ver_

bür_gen kann, als Mann von Wort ver_bür_gen kann.

6.Nun sind wir auch der Deut_schen werth, des

Vol_kes, das die Welt ver_ehrt. Hier mei_ne Hand; wir schla_gen ein, und

wol_len deut_sche Män_ner sein, und wol_len deut_sche Män_ner sein.

MERKENSTEIN

Gedicht von Joh. Bapt. Rupprecht
in Musik gesetzt von

L. van BEETHOVEN.

Op. 100.

Mässig, jedoch nicht schleppend.

Componirt im December 1814.

Zwei Singstimmen.

1. Mer _ ken _ stein! Mer _ ken _ stein! wo ich

PIANOFORTE.

p dolce

wand _ le, denk' ich dein. Wenn Au _ ro _ ra Fel _ sen rö _ thet, hell im Busch die Am _ sel

flö _ tet, wei _ dend Heer _ den sich zer _ streu'n, denk' ich dein, Mer _ ken _ stein!

f

p

1.

Merkenstein! Merkenstein!
Wo ich wandle, denk' ich dein.
Wenn Aurora Felsen röthet,
Hell im Busch die Amsel flötet,
Weidend Heerden sich zerstreu'n,
Denk' ich dein, Merkenstein!

2.

Merkenstein! Merkenstein!
Bei der schwülen Mittagspein
Sehn' ich mich nach deinen Gängen,
Deinen Grotten, Felsenhängen,
Deiner Kühlung mich zu freu'n.
Merkenstein! Merkenstein!

3.

Merkenstein! Merkenstein!
Dich erhellt mir Hesper's Schein,
Duftend rings von Florens Kränzen
Seh' ich die Gemächer glänzen,
Traulich blickt der Mond hinein.
Merkenstein! Merkenstein!

4.

Merkenstein! Merkenstein!
Dir nur hüllt die Nacht mich ein.
Ewig möcht' ich wonnig träumen
Unter deinen Schwesterbäumen,
Deinen Frieden mir verleih'n!
Merkenstein! Merkenstein!

5.

Merkenstein! Merkenstein!
Weckend soll der Morgen sein,
Lass uns dort von Ritterhöhen
Nach der Vorzeit Bildern spähen:
Sie, so gross und wir—so klein!
Merkenstein! Merkenstein!

6.

Merkenstein! Merkenstein!
Höchster Anmuth Lust_ Verein.
Ewig jung ist in Ruinen
Mir Natur in dir erschienen;
Ihr, nur ihr mich stets zu weih'n,
Denk' ich dein, Merkenstein!

DER KUSS
von C. F. Weisse.
ARIETTE
in Musik gesetzt von
L. van BEETHOVEN.
Op. 128.

Componirt im December 1822.

SCHILDERUNG EINES MÄDCHENS

in Musik gesetzt von

L. van BEETHOVEN.

Componirt im 11. Lebensjahre.

AN EINEN SÄUGLING

Gedicht von Wirths

in Musik gesetzt von

L. van BEETHOVEN.

Compouirt spätestens 1784.

ABSCHIEDSGESANG
AN WIEN'S BÜRGER
beim Auszug der Wiener Freiwilligen
Gedicht von Friedelberg
in Musik gesetzt von

L. van BEETHOVEN.

Componirt im November 1796.

Singstimme.

Entschlossen und feurig.

1. Kei _ ne   Kla _ ge soll er _ schal _ len, wenn von
2. Freun _ de!   wünscht in Sie _ ges _ tö _ nen uns zur
3. Tro _ tzend   stehn vor Don _ ner _ schlün _ den kann wohl
4. Freut euch   Vä _ ter, ju _ belt Müt _ ter! Nir _ gend,
5. Bess _ re   Men _ schen, bess _ re Bür _ ger, als wir
6. Lasst uns   fol _ gen die _ ser Fah _ ne durch The _

PIANOFORTE.

sf   sf

hier die Fah _ ne   zieht, Thrä _ nen   kei _ nem Aug' ent _ fal _ len, das im
ed _ len Rei _ se   Glück. Hei _ ter   folg' uns nach, ihr   Schö _ nen! eu _ er
auch der Bö _ se _ wicht. Mil _ den   Sinn mit Muth ver _ bin _ den, Menschheit
wo das Corps er _ scheint, nicht bei   Fein _ den, wird ihm   bit _ ter von der
nun von hin _ nen   gehn, kei _ ne   sit _ ten _ lo _ sen   Wür _ ger sollt ihr
re _ sens Kunst _ werk   reich; de _ ren   Gold _ band uns er _ mah _ ne: Tu _ gend

sf   sf   sf

Scheiden nach ihr sieht. Es ist Stolz auf diese Zierde und Ge-
seelenvoller Blick. Unsers Landes Ruhm zu mehren ziehn wir
ehren, kann er nicht. Nie das Glück der Tugend trüben, brüder-
Unschuld nachgeweint. Edel wollen wir uns rächen, schweigen
in uns wiedersehn. Unser Wien empfängt uns wieder, ruhm be-
mach' uns Fürsten gleich. Ha! wenn wir zurück sie bringen, wollen

fühl der Bürgerwürde, was auf Aller Wangen glüht, was auf
muthig hin, und kehren würdiger zu euch zurück, würdi-
lich den Landmann lieben: das ist deutscher Helden Pflicht, das ist
bis die Thaten sprechen, sie bewundre selbst der Feind, sie be-
kränzet, stark und bieder; auf! lasst hoch die Fahne wehn, auf! lasst
wir im Jubel singen: dieses Band hielt Oesterreich, dieses

Aller Wangen glüht. Es ist Stolz auf diese
ger zu euch zurück. Unsers Landes Ruhm zu
deutscher Helden Pflicht! Nie das Glück der Tugend
wundre selbst der Feind! Edel wollen wir uns
hoch die Fahne wehn! Unser Wien empfängt uns
Band hielt Oesterreich! Ha! wenn wir zurück sie

Zier _ de   und Ge _ fühl der Bür_ger _ wür_de , was auf   Al _ ler Wan _ gen
meh _ ren   ziehn wir   mu_thig hin, und   keh_ren wür_di_ger zu euch zu _
trü _ ben,   brü_der_lich den Land_mann   lie_ben: das ist   deut_scher Hel_den
rä _ chen,   schweigen   bis die Tha_ten   spre_chen, sie be _ wun_dre selbst der
wie _ der,   ruhm_be _ krän_zet, stark und   bie_der; auf! lasst   hoch die Fah _ ne
brin _ gen,   wol_len   wir im Ju_bel   sin_gen: die_ses   Band hielt Oe _ ster_

glüht,   was   auf   Al _ _ ler Wan _ gen   glüht .
rück,   wür _ di _ ger   zu euch zu _ rück.
Pflicht ,   das   ist   deut _ scher Hel _ den   Pflicht !
Feind,   sie   be _ wun _ dre selbst der   Feind !
wehn,   auf! lasst   hoch   die Fah _ ne   wehn !
reich,   die _ ses   Band   hielt Oe _ ster _ reich !

KRIEGSLIED DER OESTERREICHER

Gedicht von Friedelberg

in Musik gesetzt von

L. van BEETHOVEN.

Componirt im April 1797.

Muthig.

Singstimme.

1. Ein gro_sses deut_sches Volk sind wir, sind mäch_tig und ge-
2. Wir strei_ten nicht für Ruhm und Sold, nur für des Frie_dens
3. Mit Pi_ken, Sen_sen und Ge_schoss eilt Klein und Gross her-
4. Mann, Weib und Kind in Oe_ster_reich fühlt tief den eig_nen

PIANOFORTE.

recht. Ihr Fran_ken, das be_zwei_felt ihr? Ihr Fran_ken kennt uns
Glück! Wir keh_ren, arm an frem_dem Gold, zu un_serm Herd zu-
bei! Fürs Va_ter_land! Stimmt Klein und Gross, stimmt an das Feld_ge-
Werth. Nie, Fran_ken! wer_den wir von euch be_sie_get, nie be-

schlecht. Denn un_ser Fürst ist gut, er_ha_ben un_ser Muth! Süss
rück. Denn gu_ten Bür_gern nur blüht Se_gen der Na_tur auf
schrei! Da stehn wir un_ver_wandt für Haus und Hof und Land, mit
thört. Denn un_ser Fürst ist gut, er_ha_ben un_ser Muth! Süss

uns'rer Trau — ben Blut, und uns're Wei — ber schön; wie kann's uns bes — ser
Weinberg, Wald und Flur. Ge — recht ist un — ser Krieg; uns, uns ge — hört der
Waf — fen in der Hand, und schla — gen mu — thig drein, wie viel auch ih — rer
uns'rer Trau — ben Blut, und uns're Wei — ber schön; wie kann's uns bes — ser

Chor.

gehn, wie kann's uns bes — ser gehn? Wie kann's uns bes — ser gehn, wie
Sieg, uns, uns ge — hört der Sieg. Uns, uns ge — hört der Sieg, uns,
sein, wie viel auch ih — rer sein! Wie viel auch ih — rer sein, wie
gehn, wie kann's uns bes — ser gehn? Wie kann's uns bes — ser gehn, wie

kann's uns bes — ser gehn?
uns ge — hört der Sieg.
viel auch ih — rer sein!
kann's uns bes — ser gehn?

DER FREIE MANN

Gedicht von G. C. Pfeffel
in Musik gesetzt von

L. van BEETHOVEN.

Componirt im Jahre 1797.

1. Wer, wer ist ein frei_er Mann? Der, dem nur eig_ner Wil_le, und kei_nes Zwingherrn Gril_le Ge_se_tze ge_ben kann; der ist ein frei_er Mann! ein frei_er, frei_er Mann! Der ist ein frei_er Mann! ein frei_er, frei_er Mann!

2.

Wer ist ein freier Mann?
Der das Gesetz verehret,
Nichts thut, was es verwehret,
Nichts will, als was er kann;
Der ist ein freier Mann!

3.

Wer ist ein freier Mann?
Dem nicht Geburt noch Titel,
Nicht Sammtrock oder Kittel
Den Bruder bergen kann;
Der ist ein freier Mann!

4.

Wer ist ein freier Mann?
Der, in sich selbst verschlossen,
Der feilen Gunst der Grossen
Und Kleinen trotzen kann;
Der ist ein freier Mann!

5.

Wer ist ein freier Mann?
Der fest auf seinem Stande,
Auch selbst vom Vaterlande,
Den Undank dulden kann;
Der ist ein freier Mann!

6.

Wer ist ein freier Mann?
Der, muss er Gut und Leben
Gleich für die Freiheit geben,
Doch nichts verlieren kann;
Der ist ein freier Mann!

7.

Wer ist ein freier Mann?
Der bei des Todes Rufe
Keck auf des Grabes Stufe
Und rückwärts blicken kann;
Der ist ein freier Mann!

OPFERLIED

Gedicht von Matthisson
in Musik gesetzt von

L. van BEETHOVEN.

Langsam und feierlich.

Componirt im Jahre 1797.

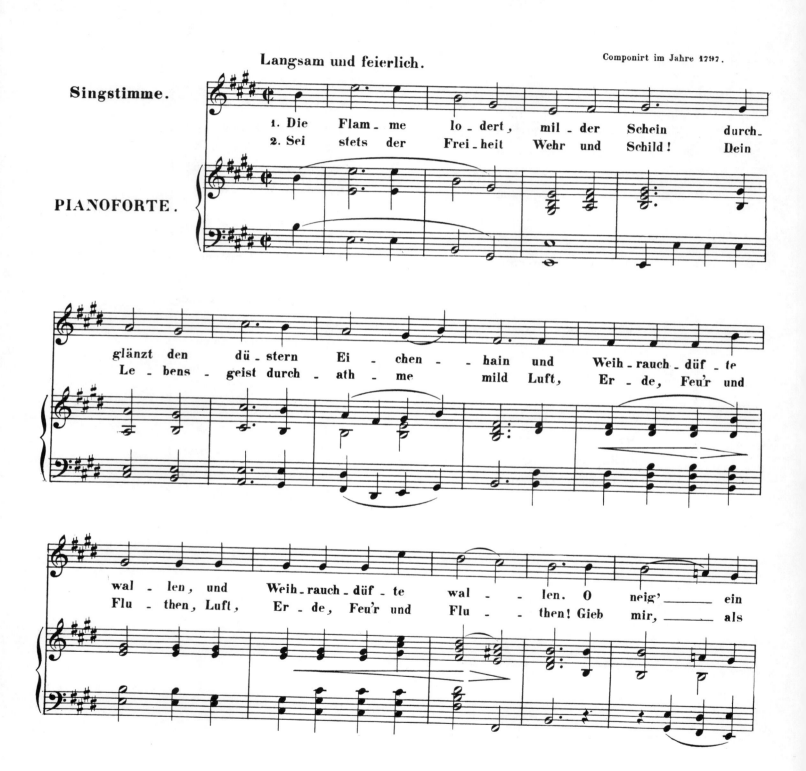

gnä - dig, ein gnä - dig Ohr zu mir; _____ und lass des Jüng - lings
Jüng - ling, als Jüng - ling und als Greis, _____ am vä - ter - li - chen

O - pfer dir, du Höch - ster, wohl - ge - fal - len, du
Herd, o Zeus, o Zeus, das Schö - ne zu dem Gu - ten, das

Höch - ster, wohl - ge - fal - len!
Schö - ne zu _____ dem Gu - ten!

DER WACHTELSCHLAG

Gedicht von S.F. Sauter

in Musik gesetzt von

L. van BEETHOVEN.

Horch, wie schallt's dor_ten so lieb_lich her_vor! Fürch_te Gott! fürch_te Gott! ruft mir die Wach_tel in's Ohr. Si_tzend im Grü_nen, von Hal_men um_hüllt, mahnt sie den Hor_cher am Saa_ten_ge_fild: lie_be

Gott! lie_be Gott!____ Er ist so gü_tig und mild, er ist so gü____tig,so

gü_tig ____ und mild.

Wie_der be_

deu____tet ihr hüpfender Schlag: lo_be Gott! lo_be Gott! der dich zu

loh__nen ver_mag.

Siehst du die herr_li_chen Früch_te im

Machen Ge-

fahren der Krieger dir bang', traue Gott! trau_e

Gott!____ sieh,__ er ver_zie_het nicht lang? Schreckt dich im Wet_ter der

Herr____ der Na_tur, bit_te Gott! bit_te

Gott! Ma_chen Ge_fah_ren der Krie_ger dir bang', trau_e

Gott! traue Gott! trau _ e Gott!___ sieh, er ver _ zie _ het nicht

lang', sieh, _ er ver _ zie _ het, ver _ zie _ het nicht lang! Bit_te Gott!

trau_e Gott! trau_e Gott! _____ sieh, er ver _ zie _ _ _ _ het, ver_zie_het nicht

lang?

ALS DIE GELIEBTE SICH TRENNEN WOLLTE

(Empfindungen bei Lydiens Untreue)

Gedicht nach dem Französischen des Soulié von St.v.Breuning.

in Musik gesetzt von

L. van BEETHOVEN.

Componirt im Jahre 1806.

Der Hoffnung letz_ter Schimmer sinkt da _ hin, sie brach die Schwü_re all' mit flücht'gem Sinn; so schwinde mir zum Trost auch immer _ dar Bewusst_sein, Be_wusst_sein, dass ich zu glück _ lich war! Was sprach ich?

Nein, von diesen meinen Ket_ten kann kein Ent_schluss, kann kei_ne Macht mich ret_ten; ach! selbst am

Ran_de der Ver _ zwei_felung bleibt e_wig, bleibt e _ wig süss mir die Er_in _ ne_rung! _

Ha! holde Hoff_nung, kehr' zu mir zu _ rü_cke, reg' all mein Feu_er auf mit einem

Bli_cke, der Lie_be Lei_den sei_en noch so gross, wer liebt, wer liebt, fühlt ganz un_

glücklich nie sein Loos!

Und du, die treu _ e Lieb' mit Kränkung

loh_net, fürcht'nicht die Brust, in der dein Bild noch wohnet, dich hassen könn _ te nie dies fühlend'

Herz, ver_ges_sen, ver_ges_sen? eh' er_liegt es sei _ nem Schmerz, eh' er_

liegt es sei _ nem, sei _ _ nem Schmerz.

poco Adagio.

a tempo.

LIED AUS DER FERNE

Gedicht von C.L.Reissig
in Musik gesetzt von

L. van BEETHOVEN.

Componirt im Jahre 1809.

Andante vivace.

PIANOFORTE.

Tanz!

cresc.   p

Poco Allegretto.

Nun treibt mich oft Sehn_sucht hin_aus auf die Höh'n, den Wunsch mei_nes

cresc.   f   p

Her_zens wo lä_cheln zu sehn! Hier sucht in der Ge_gend mein schmach_ten_der

cresc.   p

Blick, doch keh_ret er nim_mer be_frie_digt zu_rück.

cresc.-

p   cresc.   -   -

Wie klopft es im Bu_sen, als wärst du mir

p   cresc.

nah, o komm, mei_ne Hol_de, dein Jüng_ling ist da! Ich

opf_re dir al_les, was Gott mir ver_lieh, denn wie ich dich

lie_be, so liebt ich noch nie! denn wie ich dich lie_be, so

liebt ich noch nie! denn wie ich dich lie_be, so liebt ich noch nie, ja, wie

Poco Adagio.

ich dich lie_be, so liebt _____ ich noch nie! noch nie! noch nie!

NB. Man nimmt jetzt die Bewegung lebhafter als das erste Mal.

Allegretto vivace.

O Theu _ re, komm ei _ lig zum bräut _ li _ chen Tanz! _____ Ich

pfle _ _ ge schon Ro _ _ sen und Myr _ ten zum Kranz _____

Komm, komm ei _ lig, ich

pfle _ _ ge schon Ro _ _ sen und Myr _ ten zum Kranz. _____ Komm,

zau _ _ bre mein Hütt _ chen zum Tem _ pel der Ruh', _____ zum Tem _ _ pel der

DER JÜNGLING IN DER FREMDE

Gedicht von C. L. Reissig
in Musik gesetzt von

L. van BEETHOVEN.

Etwas lebhaft, doch in einer mässig geschwinden Bewegung.

Singstimme.

1. Der Früh - ling ent - blü - - het dem
2. Be - gei - stern - der Früh - - ling, du
3. Ich such - te sie Mor - - gens im
4. Da sucht' ich sie Mit - - tags, auf
5. Nun sucht' ich sie A - bends im
6. Ach Herz, dich er - kennt ja der

PIANOFORTE.

Schoos der Na - tur, mit la - - chen den Blu - men be -
heilst nicht den Schmerz! Das Le - - ben zer - drück - te mein
blü - - hen den Thal; hier tanz - - ten die Quel - len im
Blu - - men ge - streckt, im Schat - - ten von fal - len - den
ein - - sa - men Hain, die Nach - - ti - gall sang in die
Jüng - - ling nicht mehr, wie bist du so trau - rig, was

cresc.   *p*   *cresc.*

streut er die Flur: doch mir lacht ver _ ge _ bens das
fröh _ li _ ches Herz. Ach, blüht wohl auf Er _ den das für
pur _ pur _ nen Strahl, und Lie _ _ be sang schmei _ chelnd im
Blü _ then be _ deckt, ein küh _ _ len _ des Lüft _ chen um _
Stil _ le hin _ ein, und Lu _ _ na durch _ strahl _ te das
schmerzt dich so sehr? Dich quä _ _ let die Sehn _ sucht, ge _

Thal und die Höh', es bleibt mir im Bu _ sen so
mich noch die Ruh', so führ' mich dem Schoo _ se der
duf _ ten _ den Grün, doch sah' ich die lä _ cheln _ de
floss mein Ge _ sicht, doch sah' ich die schmei _ cheln _ de
Laub _ dach so schön, doch hab' ich auch hier mei _ ne
steh es mir nur, dich fes _ selt das Mäd _ chen der

bang' und so weh'.
Himm _ _ li _ schen zu.
Ru _ he nicht blühn.
Ru _ he hier nicht.
Ruh' nicht ge _ sehn!
hei _ _ mi _ schen Flur!

DER LIEBENDE

Gedicht von C.L.Reissig
in Musik gesetzt von

L. van BEETHOVEN.

In leidenschaftlicher Bewegung.

1. Welch ein wun-der-ba-res Le-ben, ein Ge-
nicht die Göt-ter-blu-me mit dem
ich die Theu-re flie-hen; Thrä-nen

misch von Schmerz und Lust, welch ein nie ge-fühl-tes Be-ben wal-tet
Hauch der Lieb' ent-glüht, sie, die in dem Hei-lig-thu-me rei-ner
zit-tern dann im Blick, und der Lie-be Gei-ster zie-hen auf der

jetzt in mei-ner Brust, wal-tet jetzt in mei-ner Brust!
Un-schuld auf-ge-blüht, rei-ner Un-schuld auf-ge-blüht?
Stel-le mich zu-rück, auf der Stel-le mich zu-rück.

Herz, mein Herz, was soll dies Po _ chen? dei _ ne Ruh' ist un _ ter _
Ja, die schö _ ne Him _ mels _ blü _ the, mit dem Zau _ berblick voll
Denn ihr pocht mit hei _ ssen Schlä _ gen e _ wig die _ ses Herz ent _

bro _ chen, sprich, was ist mit dir ge _ schehn? so hab' ich dich nie ge _ sehn, so hab'
Gü _ te, hält mit ei _ nem Band mich fest, das sich nicht zer _ rei _ ssen lässt, dass sich
ge _ gen, a _ ber ach, sie fühlt es nicht, was mein Herz im Au _ ge spricht, was mein

ich dich nie ge _ sehn, so hab' ich dich nie ge _ sehn!
nicht zer _ rei _ ssen lässt, dass sich nicht zer _ rei _ ssen lässt.
Herz im Au _ ge spricht, was mein Herz im Au _ ge spricht.

1 u. 2.   3.

2. Hat dich
3. Oft will

1 u. 2.   3.

SEHNSUCHT

Gedicht von C. L. Reissig
in Musik gesetzt von

L. van BEETHOVEN.

Mit Empfindung, aber nicht zu langsam.

Singstimme.

PIANOFORTE.

Die stil_le Nacht um_dun_kelt er_quickend Thal und Höh', der Stern der Lie_be funkelt, sanft wallend in dem See. Ver_stummt sind in den Zwei_gen die Sänger der Na_tur; ge_heimnissvolles Schweigen ruht auf der Blumenflur. Ach, mir nur schliesst kein Schlummer die müden Augen zu: Komm, lindre meinen Kummer, du stiller Gott der Ruh'! Sanft trockne mir die Thränen, gib

DES KRIEGER'S ABSCHIED

Gedicht von C.L.Reissig

in Musik gesetzt von

L. van BEETHOVEN.

denn
zärt _ lich muss der wah _ re Held stets

lass
ei _ nes deut _ schen Mäd _ chens Hand mein

denn
welch ein Lohn! wird Lieb _ chens Hand mein

und
fall' ich durch des Geg _ ners Hand, dann

sfp *rf* *p*

für ein Lieb _ chen bren _ _ nen, und doch für's Va _ ter _

Sie _ ger _ le _ ben krö _ _ nen, mein Arm ge _ hört dem

Sie _ ger _ le _ ben krö _ _ nen, mein Arm ge _ hört dem

soll mein Ruf noch tö _ _ nen: mein Arm ge _ hört dem

cresc.

land im Feld ent _ schlos _ sen ster _ ben kön _ nen.

Va _ ter _ land, mein Herz der hol _ den Schö _ nen!

Va _ ter _ land, mein Herz der hol _ den Schö _ nen!

Va _ ter _ land, mein Herz der hol _ den Schö _ nen!

p *f*

p *f* *p*

DER BARDENGEIST

Gedicht von F. R. Herrmann

in Musik gesetzt von

L. van BEETHOVEN.

Di non trattar.
Mässig langsam.

Componirt im Jahre 1813.

Singstimme.

PIANOFORTE.

1. Dort auf dem ho_hen Fel_sen

sang ein al_ter Bar_dengeist; es tönt wie Ae_ols_har_fen_klang im ban_gen schwe_ren

Trau_er_sang, der mir das Herz zer_reisst.

2.

Und wie vom Berge zart und lind
　In's süsse Blumenland
Kastalia's heil'ge Quelle rinnt:
So wallt und rauscht im Morgenwind
　Das silberne Gewand.

3.

Nur leise rauscht sein Lied dahin
　Beim grauen Dämmerschein,
Und zu den hellen Sternen hin
Entschwebt sein Herz, sein tiefer Sinn
　In süssen Träumerei'n.

4.

Und still ergriff mich mehr und mehr
　Sein wunderbares Lied.
Was siehst du Geist so bang und schwer?
Was suchst du dort im Sternenheer?
　Wie dir die Seele zieht!

5.

„Ich suche wohl, nicht find' ich mehr
　„Ach! die Vergangenheit.
„Ich sehe wohl so bang und schwer,
„Ich suche dort im Sternenheer
　„Der Deutschen goldne Zeit.

6.

„Hinunter ging die Sonne schon,
　„Kaum blieb ein Widerschein;
„Mit Arglist und mit frechem Hohn
„Pflanzt nun die düstre Nacht den Mohn
　„Um's Grab der Väter ein.

7.

„Ja, herrlich, unerschüttert, kühn
　„Stand einst der Deutsche da;
„Ach! über schwanke Trümmer ziehn
„Verhängnissvolle Sterne hin.
　„Es w a r Teutonia."

8.

Noch auf dem hohen Felsen sang
　Der alte Bardengeist;
Es tönt wie Aeol'sharfenklang
Ein banger schwerer Trauersang,
　Der mir das Herz zerreisst.

RUF VOM BERGE

Gedicht von Fr. Treitschke

in Musik gesetzt von

L. van BEETHOVEN.

Componirt am 13 December 1816.

nicht kann sein, bleib ich all _ hier.
freund _ lich auf, grüss _ test hin _ an.
klei _ nen Fuss, küss _ te wohl ihn.
Brust und Mund, fänd' ich dort Ruh.
tau _ send _ mal dein Herz ge _ schenkt.

Das letzte Mal.

2. Wenn ich ein
3. Wenn ich ein
4. Würd' ich zur
5. Geht doch kein'
6. Wohl drin _ gen

(6.) Ich nur bin fest _ ge _ bannt; wei _ ne all _ hier.

Das letzte Mal.

de _ _ _ cre _ _ scen _

_ do

Ped.

AN DIE GELIEBTE

Gedicht von J. L. Stoll

in Musik gesetzt von

L. van BEETHOVEN.

O dass ich dir vom stil - len Au - ge in sei - nem lie - be - vol - len Schein die Thrä - ne von der Wan - ge sau - ge, eh' sie die Er - de trin - ket ein!

AN DIE GELIEBTE

Gedicht von J. L. Stoll

in Musik gesetzt von

L. van BEETHOVEN.

(Frühere Bearbeitung.)

O dass ich dir vom stil_len Au_ge in sei_nem lie_be_vol_len Schein die

Thrä_ne von der Wan_ge sau_ge, eh' sie die Er_de trin_ket ein!

SO ODER SO

Gedicht von Carl Lappe

in Musik gesetzt von

L. van BEETHOVEN.

göt _ ter _ rei _ cher Him _ mel blüht! Nur Gei _ stes _ ar _ muth kann der Win _ ter
Schat _ ten vor dem Son _ nen _ brand. Nicht an das „Wo" ward Se _ lig _ keit ge _
zollt der Ast, mir nur der Zweig. Mein leich _ tes Mahl wiegt da _ rum nicht ge _
fühl und Trost für frem _ de Noth. Es strahlt der Geist nicht aus des Blu _ tes
mir er _ graut das Haar zu bald! Doch eilt nur, Lo _ cken, glän _ zend euch zu
ist der Er _ de Glück und Noth. Zu kur _ zer Tag! Zu schnell ver _ rauscht das

V.5.
(Etwas verzögernd.)

V.5.
(Erstes Zeitmaass.)

mor _ den: Kraft fügt zu Kraft, und Glanz zu Glanz der Nor _ den. Nord o _ der Süd!
bun _ den; wer hat das Glück schon au _ sser sich ge _ fun _ den? Stadt o _ der Land!
rin _ ge; Lust am Ge _ nuss be _ stimmt den Werth der Din _ ge. Arm o _ der reich!
Wel _ le, ein an _ drer Spie _ gel brennt in Son _ nen _ hel _ le. Blass o _ der roth!
fär _ ben, es ist nicht Scha _ de, Sil _ ber zu er _ wer _ ben. Jung o _ der alt!
Le _ ben! Wa _ rum so schön und doch so rasch ver _ schwe _ ben? Schlaf o _ der Tod!

cre _ scen _ do   f   p

V.6.
(Erstes Zeimaass.)

wenn nur die See _ le glüht!
die Au _ ssen _ welt ist Tand!
die Glück _ li _ chen sind reich!
nur nicht das Au _ ge todt!
doch erst im Gra _ be kalt!
hell strahlt das Mor _ gen _ roth!

Ped.

DAS GEHEIMNISS

Gedicht von Wessenberg

in Musik gesetzt von

L. VAN BEETHOVEN.

Wo blüht das Blümchen, das nie ver_blüht? Wo strahlt das Sternlein, das

e _ wig glüht? Dein Mund, o Mu_se! dein heil'ger Mund thu' mir das

Blüm_chen und Stern_lein kund, thu' mir das Blümchen und Stern_lein kund.

RESIGNATION

Gedicht von P. Graf v. Haugwitz

in Musik gesetzt von

L. van BEETHOVEN.

ABENDLIED
unter'm gestirnten Himmel
Gedicht von H.Goeble
in Musik gesetzt von
L. van BEETHOVEN.

Schaut so gern nach je _ nen Ster _ nen, wie zu _ rück in's Va _ ter _ land, hin nach

je _ nen lich _ ten Fer _ nen, und ver _ gisst der Er _ de Tand; will nur rin _ gen, will nur

stre _ ben, ih _ rer Hül _ le zu ent _ schwe _ ben: Er _ de ist ihr eng'und

klein, auf den Ster _ nen möcht' sie sein.

Ob der Er _ de Stür _ me to _ ben, fal _ sches Glück den Bö _ sen lohnt: hof _ fend bli _ cket sie nach o _ ben, wo der Ster _ nen _ rich _ _ ter thront. Kei _ ne Furcht kann sie mehr quä _ len, kei _ ne Macht kann ihr be _ feh _ len; mit ver _ klärtem An _ ge _ sicht schwingt sie sich zum Him _ mels _ licht.

ANDENKEN

Gedicht von Matthisson

in Musik gesetzt von

L. van BEETHOVEN.

je _ der Fer _ ne denk' ich nur dein, denk' ich nur dein! O den _ ke, o

den _ ke mein, o den _ ke mein, bis zum Ver _ ein auf besserm Ster _ ne! In je _ der

Fer _ ne denk' ich nur dein, denk' ich nur dein, denk' ich nur dein, nur dein, nur

dein, nur dein, nur dein! ja _____ nur dein, nur dein!

ICH LIEBE DICH

Gedicht von Herrosee
in Musik gesetzt von

L. van BEETHOVEN.

Ich lie_be dich, so wie du mich, am A_bend und am Mor_gen, noch war kein Tag, wo du und ich nicht theil_ten uns're Sor_gen. Auch wa_ren sie für dich und mich ge_theilt leicht zu er_tra_gen; du trö_ste_test im Kum_mer mich, ich weint' in dei_ne Kla_gen, in dei_ne

SEHNSUCHT

Gedicht von Goethe

viermal in Musik gesetzt von

L. van BEETHOVEN.

N° 1.

Andante poco Adagio.

Nº 2.

Poco Andante.

1. Nur wer die Sehn_sucht kennt weiss, was ich lei _ _
2. Ach! der mich liebt und kennt ist in der Wei _ _

de ! Al _ lein und ab _ ge _ trennt von al _ ler Freu _ de,
te . Es schwin_delt mir, es brennt mein Ein _ ge _ wei _ de.

cresc.

seh' ich an's Fir _ ma _ ment nach je _ ner Sei _ _ te.
Nur wer die Sehn_sucht kennt weiss, was ich lei _ _ de!

cresc.

Nº 3.

Poco Adagio.

1. Nur wer die Sehn_sucht kennt weiss, was ich lei _ de! Al _
2. Ach! der mich liebt und kennt ist in der Wei _ te. Es

lein und ab _ ge _ trennt von al _ ler Freu _ _ _ de,
schwin _ delt mir, es brennt mein Ein _ ge _ wei _ _ _ de.

seh' ich an's Fir _ ma _ ment nach je _ ner Sei _ te.
Nur wer die Sehn _ sucht kennt weiss, was ich lei _ de!

N.° 4.

Assai Adagio.

1. Nur wer die Sehn_sucht kennt weiss, was ich lei _ de! Al_

lein und ab _ ge _ trennt von al _ ler Freu_de, seh' ich an's Fir_ma _ ment ___ nach je_ner Sei _

te. 2. Ach! der mich liebt und kennt ist in der Wei _ _ te. Es schwin_delt

mir, es brennt mein Ein _ ge_wei _ _ de. ___ Nur wer die Sehnsucht kennt

weiss, was ich lei _ de, ja, weiss, was ich lei _ _ de!

LA PARTENZA
(DER ABSCHIED)
Gedicht von Metastasio
in Musik gesetzt von
L. van BEETHOVEN.

Ec_co quel fie_ro i_stan _ te! Ni_ce, mia Ni_ce, ad_di _ o! Co_me vi_vrò, ben
Das ist die Schreckensstun _ de, ha! meine Lip_pen be _ ben, wie kann ich Armer

mi_o, co _ sì lon_tan da te? Io vi_vrò sempre in
le _ ben, o Ni _ ce, fern von dir? Le _ ben muss ich in

pe _ ne, io non a_vrò più be_ne, e tu, chi sa se mai ti sov_ve_rai di
Lei_den, oh _ ne dich flieh'n die Freuden, und du, wirst du auch schenken ein lie _ bend Sehnen

me, e tu, chi sa se mai ti sov_ve_rai di me!
mir? und du, wirst du auch schenken ein lie_bend Sehnen mir?

IN QUESTA TOMBA OSCURA

Gedicht von Gius. Carpani.

in Musik gesetzt von

L. van BEETHOVEN.

men ——— e non e non ba-gnar mie
Herz ——— und be ne — — tze wei nend mei ne

ce ne_ri d'in_u_ti_le ve len. In que_sta, in
A_sche nicht mit eit lem, eit lem Schmerz. In die_sem, in

questa tom_ba o_scura la scia-mi ri_po_sar; quando vi_ve_vo, in_gra_ta, do_
diesem dunklen Grabe lass—— entschlummert mich sein! als ich auf Er_den war, Falsche, o

ve_vi a me pen_sar, a me pen_sar, in_gra_ta, in_gra ta!
dachtest da du mein! du mein, du mein! du treulos fal_sches Herz!

SEUFZER EINES UNGELIEBTEN
UND
GEGENLIEBE

Gedichte von G. A. Bürger
in Musik gesetzt von

L. van BEETHOVEN.

(Nachgelassenes Werk.)

Seufzer eines Ungeliebten.

mir, au _ _ sser mir, ja al_les au _ _ sser

mir! Wenn gleich im Hain, auf Flur und Mat_ten sich Baum und Staude, Moos und Kraut durch

Lie _ be und Ge _ gen _ lie _ be gatten; vermählt sich mir doch kei_ne Braut, doch kei _ ne

Braut. Wenn gleich im Hain,auf Flur und Mat_ten sich Baum und Stau_de, Moos und Kraut durch

Gegenliebe.

Wüsst' ich, wüsst' ich,

Allegretto.

wüsst'ich, wüsst'ich, dass du mich lieb und

werth ein bis_chen hiel_test, und von dem, was ich für dich, nur ein Hundert_theil_chen

fühl_test; dass dein Dank hübsch mei_nem Gruss hal_ben Wegs ent_ge_gen kä_me, und dein

Mund den Wech_sel_kuss ger_ne gäb' und wie_der näh_me: dann, o

Himmel, au_sser sich, wür_de ganz mein Herz zer _ lo _ dern! Leib und Le _ ben könnt' ich dich nicht ver_

gebens las_sen fodern! Ge_gen_gunst er _ hö _ het Gunst,

Lie_be nähret Ge _ gen _ lie_be, und ent_flammt zur Feu_ers_brunst, was ein

Aschen_fünkchen blie_be, und ent _ flammt zur Feu_ers_brunst, was ein Aschen fünkchen blie _ be.

Him_mel, au_sser sich, wür_de ganz mein Herz zer _ lo_dern! Leib und

Le _ ben könnt' ich dich nicht ver _ ge_bens las_sen fo_dern!

Ge _ gen_gunst er_hö_het Gunst,

Lie_be näh_ret Ge_gen _ lie_be, und ent_

DIE LAUTE KLAGE

Gedicht von Herder
in Musik gesetzt von

L. van BEETHOVEN.

(Nachgelassenes Werk.)

Lie_be! Sie gab dir die lau_te Jam_mer_kla_ge zum Trost, zum Trost, mir den ver_

stum_men_den Gram! Ach, die hart_ver_thei_len_de Lie_be! Sie gab dir die

lau_te Jam_mer_kla_ge zum Trost,____ zum Trost, mir den ver_stum_men_den

Gram, mir, mir den ver_stum_men_den Gram!